Ayatollah al-Udhma Sayyid Sadiq Shirazi

The Guide to Hajj Rites

The Rulings and Procedures of Hajj

D1364820

Translated by
Z. Olyabek

Bismillah al-Rahmaan al-Raheem

It is the duty to Allah incumbent on those who can, to make the pilgrimage to the House. But with respect to those disbelieve, Allah has no need of all mankind.

The Holy Qur'an, The Family of 'Emran (3): 97

Bismillah al-Rahmaan al-Raheem

Acting in accordance with this *risalah* "Manaasik al-Hajj" is qualifying and discharges the duty by the will of Allah Almighty.

Sadiq al-Shirazi

Contents

Translators' Foreword

This book is the English translation of the *Manaasik al-Hajj*, 2nd printing, 1422 H / 2002 CE. The order of the material in this English version has been kept the same as the Arabic original.

The book consists of main parts; the Hajj rulings, and the Hajj procedure. For the English translation, a third part – glossary – has been added for the benefit.

PART 1 deals with the Hajj **rulings** in general and also addresses such topics as the eligibility of an individual for the Hajj, and defines "the ability" one is required to attain in order for him/her to be considered eligible. In addition this part also addresses the issues and Hajj rulings of Hajj by Proxy, Hajj by Grant, etc.

PART 2 of this work presents detailed **procedures** for performing the Hajj in a step-by-step fashion, starting from the rite needed and the site at which it must be performed, up to the final one. To begin with, a brief overview of the entire process is outlined such that the reader would obtain an overall idea of the process involved. Specific issues concerning women are also dealt with where applicable.

PART 3 is a **glossary** of the technical terminologies and Arabic words used in this text, which has been compiled by the translator. This has been included, at the end of the book, to help the reader easily find the meaning and explanation of the Arabic terms and words used in this text.

Finally a number of points should be taken into account when reading this work:

When performing an act of worship is referred to as a *mostahab* precaution, it means that the pilgrim has the option as whether or not to do that act, although one is encouraged to do so. On the other hand, if performing an act is based on obligatory precaution, then it is obligatory for the pilgrim to act accordingly while having the option to refer to the *fatwa* of another *marje'* (authority) in respect of this act.

All technical terminologies and Arabic words are given lower case and *italic*, whereas names of places are given in title case and non-italic. A glossary of all such terms is presented in part 3 of the book.

To avoid ambiguity, and for the sake of clarity, the reader should note that word Haram refers to the precinct or area that encompasses the holy city of Makkah. This word should be distinguished from the word *haraam*, which means prohibited. Not that the same word is also used in the term 'Masgid al-Haraam' referring to holy mosque in Makkah that encompasses the holy Ka'bah.

References to masculine pronouns such as *he* and *his* are applicable to both sexes where appropriate. This is to avoid the tedious repetition of *he/she, his/her,* etc. Similarly the word *Pilgrim* refers to both male and female pilgrims.

All the terms and expressions within [ ] are the translator's, as well as all the explanatory footnotes.

Z. Olyabek
Dhil-Qa'dah 1423
January 2003

Introduction

Bismillah al-Rahmaan al-Raheem

Praise is to the Lord of the Worlds, and Blessings and Peace is upon Muhammad and his pure and impeccable progeny, and curse is upon all of their enemies.

This book is the translation of the *work* "Manaasik al-Hajj", explaining the various issues of Hajj together with its rulings and rites.

Before dealing with the rulings of Hajj it would be appropriate to present some of the *hadith* narrated about the significance of Hajj.

Rasulollah *salla-llahu-alayhi-wa-aalih* said,

"The Hajj has Paradise as its reward, and the Umrah is atonement for all sins".[1]

Imam Zayn al-'Abidin *alayhis-salaam* said,

"Perform Hajj and Umrah, for your bodies will be healthy, your sustenance will be increased, and the expenses of your families will be met."[2]

Imam Zayn al-'Abidin *alayhis-salaam* also said,

"The pilgrim is forgiven, Paradise is [made] compulsory for him, the good deed is continued for him, and his family and wealth are protected."[3]

Imam Baqir *alayhis-salaam* said,

"Islam has been built on five [aspects]: on *Salaat* (the daily prayers), *Zakat* (the monetary contributions), *Hajj* (pilgrimage), *Sawm* (fasting),

---

[1] *al-Kaafi,* vol. 4, p 253
[2] *al-Kaafi,* vol. 4, p 252
[3] *Wasaa'el al-Shi'a,* vol. 11, p 9

9

and the *Wilaayah* (the authority and guardianship of the Ahl-ul-Bayt), and nothing is as important as the *Wilaayah*."[4]

Imam Sadiq *alayhis-salaam* said,

"The pilgrim continues to have the Light of Allah upon him so long as he does not sin."[5]

Imam Sadiq *alayhis-salaam* also said,

"If you spend one *Dirham* for the Hajj is better than spending twenty thousand *Dirham* in a good cause."[6]

Imam Sadiq *alayhis-salaam* also said,

"If one dies and has not performed Hajjat-al-Islam, while a need, sickness, or a Ruler does not prevent him, let him die as a Jew or a Christian."[7]

This is in addition to the fact that Hajj is one of the fundamental principles of Islam, and its obligation, while meeting the prescribed criteria, is amongst the necessities of religion, and abandoning it is a great sin.

---

[4] *al-Kaafi*, vol. 2, p 18
[5] *Wasaa'el al-Shi'a*, vol. 11, p 98
[6] *al-Kaafi*, vol. 4, p 255
[7] *Man La Yadheroho al-Faqih*, vol. 2, p 447

PART 1 – The Categories of Hajj

1. The Hajj is either obligatory or *mostahab* (desirable, optional), and the obligatory Hajj is classified in three categories:

I. *Hajjat-al-Islam,* which is obligatory upon the individual when s/he meets all the prescribed criteria, which shall be mentioned shortly *InSha'Allah.* According to the fundamentals of Islam, the Hajj is not obligatory except once.

II. The Hajj that becomes obligatory through *nadhr* (vow), promise, and oath.

III. The Hajj that becomes obligatory by proxy, thorough the hiring of agents.

As for the *mostahab* Hajj, it is any Hajj other than the above.

The Conditions of Obligation of Hajjat-al-Islam

2. The conditions that if met make *Hajjat-al-Islam* obligatory are five:

a. Adolescence,
b. Sanity of the mind,
c. Freedom,
d. Ability – to be able to afford going to the Hajj and come back, as well as leaving behind enough for his family to live on, "Returning to Sufficient" means of living.
e. Absence of hindrance on the way [to the Hajj].

3. The obligation of the Hajj is immediate when its requirements are all met. That is, if the individual meets all the preconditions and prerequisites of the Hajj – thus considered "able" and "eligible", or in technical terms *mostatee'* [8] – it becomes compulsory upon him [to go to Hajj] in the same year of eligibility, and it is not permissible for him to

---

[8] This meeting of the all preconditions and prerequisites is referred to as *mostatee'* literally meaning "able".

delay [going to Hajj]. Delaying the Hajj without having a valid [Islamically] legal reason constitutes a sin, and [from then onwards] the Hajj remains "established" as his responsibility [regardless of his ability or the lack of it]. It is mandatory for him to perform the Hajj in the following year [and if not] as soon as possible.

4. It is obligatory upon the *mostatee'* to prepare all the necessary means and requirements of the Hajj journey in the first year of his ability/eligibility, even if they were many and lengthy.

5. It is obligatory upon the individual going to Hajj to learn the Hajj rites and rulings.

6. If it is not possible for him to go to Hajj on his own, he may choose a group that he trusts to go with, and if there are many groups that he trusts, it would not be obligatory for him to go with the first one. If he travelled with other than the first one, but, due to certain circumstances, he did not manage to get to the Hajj; if in the future, he were not to meet all the prerequisites of the Hajj, he would not be regarded as having committed disobedience, nor the Hajj remains "established" in his responsibility.

7. If he travelled with a group that he is not sure of, and it happened that he did not get to Hajj, he has sinned, and the Hajj remains "established" in his responsibility. It is obligatory for him to perform the Hajj in the following year, or as soon as possible.

The Hajj of Underage Children

8. It is desirable for the underage child, who distinguishes [the good and the bad], to perform the Hajj, and the validity of the Hajj is conditional upon the permission of his guardian such as his father. If he met all the criteria for Hajj other than that of adolescence, his Hajj is correct, but it would not qualify as *Hajjat-al-Islam* [and therefore when s/he is at or over the adolescence age, s/he is obliged to go to Hajj whenever becoming *mostatee'*].

9. If the under aged distinguishing child went on the Hajj [journey] but reached adolescence before declaring and assuming *ihraam*, and if he met all criteria to be considered as *mostatee'*, his Hajj is correct and qualifies as *Hajjat-al-Islam*.

10. If one performed the Hajj with the *mostahab* intention, believing that he is not adolescent, but then it became apparent that he is, his Hajj is correct and qualifies as *Hajjat-al-Islam*, unless that his Hajj has been considered with the specific intention of *mostahab* such that if the Hajj is considered to be obligatory for him he would not perform it, which is an extremely rare supposition.

11. It is *mostahab* – desirable – for the guardian of the non-distinguishing child – male or female – to wear him the two garments of *ihraam*, after removing his normal clothing, and dictate to him the *talbiyah* word by word. If it is not possible to dictate the wordings to the child, the guardian should intend and say it on the child's behalf, and he should prevent the child from committing prohibited acts of the *ihraam*. He should help the child perform any rite of the Hajj if he could do so, or do it on his behalf if the child could not do so. The father should take him to do the *tawaaf* around the House, the *sa'y*, observe the *woquf* in Arafaat and Mash'ar al-Haraam, go to Mina, perform the stoning, shaving or trimming, and all other rites of the Hajj such as prayer of the tawaaf, etc.

12. The expenses of the child should come out of the child's own assets, unless that would leave him penniless, in which case it is the guardian's responsibility.

13. The cost of the *Had'y* should be from the assets of the child, and if latter did not have any, should come out of his guardian's, and he should offer the *Had'y* by proxy on the child's behalf.

14. The *kaffaarah* of hunting, if the child committed it, is from the assets of the guardian if the guardian was the father, or from the assets of the child if the guardian was not the father. However, the *kaffaarah* [of committing prohibited acts] other than hunting is from the wealth of the child regardless of the guardian being the father or not.

15. If the *kaffaarah* were to be paid from the assets of the child, if the guardian deducted them from the wealth of the child it is sufficient, otherwise, it is obligatory upon the child to deduct them from his assets after the age of adolescence.

The Mind

16. The insane, even if the insanity was periodical – i.e. insanity appears on certain occasions – is not obliged to the Hajj, unless he was *mostatee'* and able to perform most of the rites of the Hajj – including the fundamental rites of the Hajj – in his state of sanity. In that case he is obliged to perform the Hajj. The same ruling applies to an individual who is in a state of unconsciousness.

Freedom

17. The slave – male or female – is not obliged to the Hajj even if s/he was *mostatee'* and had the permission of the master. If with the permission of the master, his *mostahab* Hajj is correct, but this would not qualify as *Hajjat-al-Islam*. If they were freed and were *mostatee'* they would then be obliged to the *Hajjat-al-Islam*.

Freedom of passage

18. One of the conditions of the obligation of the Hajj is the freedom of the passage, and absence of hindrance en route to the Hajj. If there were a danger threatening the life of the individual, his family or his assets and possessions, he would not be obliged to the Hajj. Similarly if there was a religious prohibition, such as if [the performance of] the Hajj would result in abandoning a more important obligation such as a mandatory jihad [which the individual is liable to], or committing a disobedience the repercussion of which is greater than the outcome of the Hajj, then the Hajj is not obligatory upon him.

19. One of the conditions of the obligation of the Hajj is the availability of enough time to perform the rites of the Hajj. If one met all the criteria for the Hajj at a time when he would not be able to get there in time, or he

would manage to get there but with great difficulty that is normally unbearable, then the Hajj is not obligatory upon him.

Physical ability

20. Physical ability is one of the criteria of the obligation of the Hajj. Thus if one was ill, or had lost a limb, or too old such that he would not be able to perform the Hajj himself, it is obligatory for him to perform the Hajj by proxy, i.e. to appoint someone else to perform the Hajj on his behalf, if he has met other criteria required for the obligation of the Hajj.

21. The individual who was financially able, if he was also physically able, it would be obligatory for him to perform the Hajj himself, and it would not be sufficient if someone else performs the Hajj on his behalf, whether voluntarily or by hire. In the case of a *mostahab* Hajj, however, if someone performs the Hajj on his behalf, it would be correct.

The expenses cover

22. One of the conditions of the obligation of the Hajj, is the availability of the expenses to cover for the journey [to the Hajj], and back – both for the trip and living expenses – according to his social status, even by the minimum amount. If he does not have both, the Hajj is not obligatory upon him.

23. The criteria for the amount of the expenses are that he should have available to him from the place where he wants to depart from. For example if one went on business trip to Medina or Jeddah and it coincided with the Hajj season, and he was able to provide for the expenses from there, the Hajj would be obligatory for him, even if he would not be able to cover the expenses if it were from his hometown.

24. If providing the expenses means selling something he owns at a less-than-normal price, and selling it would not put him in difficulty, it would be obligatory for him to sell and perform the Hajj with the proceed. However, if selling the item(s) would put him in difficulty, the Hajj would not be obligatory upon him.

25. If the costs of the Hajj expenses temporarily increased in one of the years, such that they would go back to normal afterwards, if paying the extra cost does not put him in difficulty, it is not permitted for him to delay the Hajj, and the Hajj becomes obligatory upon him in the same year.

26. The ability to provide for the expenses is conditional on covering the cost of the trip there and back, and during his stay in Makkah, but if he wanted to reside in Makkah permanently, providing the cost of the journey back is not conditional for him.

Return to Sufficiency

27. Return to Sufficiency is another prerequisite in the obligation of the Hajj, which means that when he returns back home from Hajj he should have [or be in] a position to manage himself and his family, actually and potentially. Thus if he does not have [a surplus sum] other than the capital with which he runs his and his family's affairs, such that if he spends that capital for the Hajj, he would come back with no sufficient [funds to manage his family], the Hajj would not be obligatory for him.

28. It is not obligatory to sell the basic essentials of life, such as the house, furniture or clothing that fit his status, even books in the case of students, to use the proceeds to go to Hajj. However, if he had things superfluous to his need, such as having two houses, for one of which he has no need, it is obligatory for him to sell the [second] house in order to go to Hajj. The same is applicable to other superfluous stuff.

29. If something is no longer considered as essential, such as jewellery for a woman who either no longer wears them and it is not befitting for her status to keep them, or if she has grown old and it is not customary for her to wear them, if the proceeds of the sale would be sufficient for the Hajj, it would be obligatory for her to sell them and go to Hajj.

30. If he owned a house, and also had a house under his control such that he would be able to live in the latter house with his family without any difficulty or finding himself morally obliged to the owner of the house, it

16

is not obligatory for him to sell the house he owns to go to Hajj. However, if he and his family were living in the house under his control, such that normally he is not considered to need the house he owns, it would be obligatory for him to sell his house to go to Hajj. The same ruling apply to other things too if the sale proceeds cover the Hajj expenses.

31. If he had sufficient funds for the Hajj expenses, but he was not married yet, or he did not have a house to live in, or does not have the furniture for the house, the obligation of the Hajj has a higher priority. Unless his remaining unmarried, or without a house to live in, or without furniture constitutes such difficulty that he would not normally bear, in which case the Hajj is not obligatory for him.

Borrowing

32. If one does not have the fund [to go to the Hajj], but can borrow [the amount], it is *mostahab* for him to perform the Hajj through borrowing. [although this would not qualify for Hajjat-al-Islam.]

33. If one was [potentially] able to borrow sufficient money to go to Hajj, it is not obligatory for him to borrow. Furthermore, if one borrowed the money, the Hajj would not be obligatory for him, even if he would be able to pay the money back afterwards.

34. If one does not have sufficient fund available to him for the Hajj expenses, but someone owes him some money that would be sufficient for the purpose, and the time for the payment is due, it is obligatory for him to ask him [the debtor] for the money, and use it for the purpose of the Hajj. Furthermore, if the payment time is not due, but if the debtor were to realise that the individual need the money for the Hajj and he would give him the money, it is also obligatory for him to ask the debtor for the money to use it for the Hajj. If the debtor would not deal with the matter amicably, and the creditor could use the offices or mediation of a third party to get the money for him, it is obligatory for him to do so and use the money for the purpose of the Hajj.

35. If the debtor denied the debt, it would be obligatory upon the creditor to take his case to the court of law – even if non-Islamic – to prove his right and recover the debt, in order to use it for the purpose of the Hajj. If the debtor could not pay him back, or if the debtor denied the debt and the creditor could not force him to pay him back, or forcing debtor would be difficult for creditor, or if the debt payment is not due yet and the debtor would not pay him if he asked him, the Hajj would not be obligatory for him.

36. If one had in his possession enough fund for the purpose of the Hajj, but at the same time he also owed [others] money, such that if he went to Hajj he would not be able to pay back his debt, the Hajj would not be obligatory for him, regardless of whether his debt is due now or in the future, and whether the debt was prior to obtaining that money or following it. However, if he would be able to repay the debt when it is due, the Hajj would be obligatory for him.

37. If he had enough money for the purpose of Hajj, but he was in debt in terms of the Religious taxes, such as Khums, Zakat, *kaffaaraat* such that if he paid those dues he would not be able to go to Hajj, it is obligatory for him to pay his dues, rather than going to Hajj.

38. If anyone of certain skill or expertise, who lives off his skill or expertise, inherits a sum that is sufficient for the Hajj purpose, as well as for his family while he is on the Hajj trip, he would be obliged to the Hajj.

39. If one, because of his poverty, receives payments from the Religious taxes such as the Khums and Zakat, inherits a sufficient sum, it is obligatory for him to refrain from accepting those payments, and it is not obligatory for him to go to Hajj with the amount he had inherited. Unless the amount he inherited is such that it would prevent him from accepting payments as well as enabling him to go to the Hajj, in which case the Hajj would be obligatory for him.

40. The Hajj is not obligatory for an individual that, if he wanted to go to the Hajj, he would have to spend everything that he owns to the extent

that he would be destitute, even though it would then be possible for him to survive by accepting donation collected for the poor, for example.

Miscellaneous issues

41. If one performed the Hajj as a rambler, or with someone else's money, his Hajj qualifies. If he performed the Hajj with usurped money, his Hajj would be void, and he has committed a sin. However, if he obtained the two garments of *ihraam*, his clothing during the Tawaaf and Sa'y, and the cost of the Had'y from legal money, his Hajj would be correct, although he has sinned in dealing with the usurped money and this Hajj would not be accepted from him.

42. It is not obligatory to attain the ability [i.e. become *mostatee'*] to go to Hajj by means of trading and saving. Also it is not obligatory to accept a gift [of a sum of money] from a donor to go to Hajj with, nor is it obligatory to accept to do a service or a job for a wage sufficient to go to Hajj, even if that service or job was befitting to his status. Of course, if he did one of those things and obtained a sum sufficient for the Hajj, the Hajj would be obligatory for him.

43. If one accepted to work in a group travelling to the Hajj, for a wage that would be sufficient for the Hajj such that he would be considered as able – *mostatee'* – if his work does not contravene the execution of the rites of Hajj, it would be obligatory for him to perform the Hajj that year. However, if his work would contravene carrying out the rites of his Hajj, and for example he would not be able to observe the *woquf* in Arafaat and Mash'ar, say, the Hajj would not be obligatory for him that year. Furthermore, it would not be obligatory for him to save the money to perform the Hajj next year. If the money remained in his possession until the following year, and it was sufficient for the Hajj, the Hajj would be obligatory for him.

44. If one agreed to do the Hajj by proxy [on behalf of someone else] for a fee, and with that fee he too was considered *mostatee'* – able and liable to perform the Hajj, for example, the fee was sufficient for performing two rounds of Hajj, if the assignor does not specify the Hajj to be

performed in the current year, then it would be obligatory for him to perform the Hajj on behalf of himself first, and perform the Hajj by proxy in the following year. If the Hajj by proxy was specified or dedicated to be for the current year, it would be obligatory for him to perform the Hajj by proxy first, and the obligation of the Hajj for him ceases to be valid, unless the fee [he earned] remained in his possession until the following year and was sufficient for the Hajj.

45. If one had some money but was not sure as to whether it was sufficient for the Hajj, because he was not sure of the cost of the Hajj, or he knew the cost of the Hajj but not sure of the amount he has, it would be obligatory for him to find out in each case.

46. If one had sufficient money for the Hajj, but the money was not within his access, if he was able to obtain the money – without unusual difficulty or harm – even by seeking others' help etc. the Hajj would be obligatory for him. If however, he was not able to obtain his money in any way, the Hajj would not be obligatory for him so long as his access [to the money] was excused.

47. If one obtained a sum of money that was sufficient for the Hajj, but it was not in time for the Hajj, it is not obligatory for him to save for the following Hajj season, and it is permissible for him to use that money for his need, or give it to others, or give it as a gift to whoever he wished. If it remained in his possession until the next Hajj season, the Hajj would be obligatory for him.

48. If the money that was sufficient for the Hajj was lost, whether before the trip to Hajj, during it, or after it, this renders him not *mostatee'*, i.e. unable to perform the Hajj, and the Hajj is not obligatory upon him. If he regains that ability afterwards, he would then be liable to the Hajj.

49. If due to an oversight, one forgot that he had sufficient sum to go to Hajj, or due to an oversight one did not realise that he was liable to Hajj, and he did not notice his oversight until after the loss of the money or after the Hajj season, he would not be considered liable to Hajj if he was not negligent – *moqassir* – in his oversight. Of course if the sum

remained in his possession until the following year, the Hajj would then be obligatory upon him.

50. If one performed the Hajj while he is not *mostatee'* – i.e. not meeting all the preconditions required before being liable to perform the Hajj – this Hajj would not qualify for *Hajjat-al-Islam*. If at a later date he became *mostatee'*, he would still be liable to the Hajj. The same is applicable, if he was assigned to perform the Hajj on behalf of someone else.

51. If one did not believe that he meets the preconditions of the Hajj, i.e. he is *mostatee'*, and performed a *mostahab* Hajj with the intention of complying with his duties he is liable to, and then he discovered that he was actually *mostatee'*, this Hajj would be qualified as *Hajjat-al-Islam*. However, if the intention was specified to be *mostahab* only such that if the Hajj turned out to be obligatory to him he would not have performed it, then this Hajj would not qualify for *Hajjat-al-Islam*, and he would be obliged to the Hajj if he became *mostatee'*.

52. It is desirable – *mostahab* –for an individual who has performed the *Hajjat-al-Islam* to perform Hajj for the second, third, fourth time, and so on. It is also desirable for one to perform the Hajj on behalf of others voluntarily, or perform the *tawaaf* and its prayer on their behalf, whether they are alive or dead. Furthermore it is also desirable to perform the Hajj on behalf of the Ma'soomeen *alayhum-as-salam*, an act that is very emphasised and extremely *mostahab*.

53. If a non-Shi'a embraced and followed the teachings of Ahl-ul-Bayt *alayhum-as-salam* and became a "Shi'a", if he had performed the Hajj according to his *madhhab* (the teachings of his sect), even though it may not be correct according to ours, or if he had performed the Hajj according to our *madhhab*, even though it may not be according to his, that Hajj qualifies and he is not obliged to repeat the Hajj again. However, if he had performed the Hajj incorrectly; both according to his *madhhab* or according to ours, that Hajj would not qualify and he remains obliged to repeat.

Hajj by Grant

54. Just as one can meet the prerequisites for qualifying for the Hajj through his own possessions and wealth, those preconditions are also met by receiving a grant that is sufficient for the expenses of the Hajj. This is so regardless of the number of donors [of the grant], or whether the donor(s) arranged for the journey to and from, or forfeited the cost, or in any other way and arrangement. The recipient is considered – *mostatee'* – able and liable to the Hajj, and it is obligatory for him to perform the Hajj in the same year and that would qualify for the *Hajjat-at-Islam*.

55. If performing the Hajj would not affect the means of living and sustenance of the recipient concerned, then he is obliged to perform the Hajj. Otherwise, if performing the Hajj would affect his means of living after he returns, like if he earned his year-long income during the Hajj season [in his hometown], and if he were to perform the Hajj he would have missed that opportunity [of earning for the year, he would therefore not be obliged to Hajj], since Return to Sufficiency is one of the preconditions of the Hajj.

56. If an individual granted another a sum that is sufficient for going to Hajj with, but he did not make it conditional to go to Hajj with, the recipient is not obliged to accept it, and thus he is not obliged to Hajj. However, if he accepted the sum, he would be obliged to Hajj since he became *mostatee'*.

57. If an individual granted another a sum that is sufficient for going to Hajj with, and made it conditional to go to Hajj with, or if he gave him the option of either going to Hajj or elsewhere, the recipient is obliged to accept and to Hajj, since with that [donation] he became *mostatee'*. Unless, however, in accepting the donation there is a difficulty or the recipient would find himself morally obliged to the donor, in which case it is not obligatory for him to accept.

58. If one became *mostatee'* through grant or donation, and if he also owed money, if his going to Hajj would not hinder him from paying off his debt, or if it did the creditor would put up with the delay, it is

22

obligatory for him to accept the offer [of the donation] and perform the Hajj. However, if his going to Hajj would hinder him from paying back his debt, or the creditor would not agree to the delay, then he would not be obliged to accept [the offer of donation] nor to Hajj.

59. If one donated a sum to a group so that one of them could go to Hajj, if one of that group rushed to him [to accept the grant] he would be obliged to the Hajj, but the rest would not. If no one rushed to him and they were all able to go to the Hajj – [with the exception of the financial ability] – they would all continue to be obliged to go to Hajj [until one of them opts to accept the offer, when this obligation would be annulled for the rest].

60. As a result of a donation, the recipient becomes liable to the Hajj, which he must discharge as a duty. Thus if an individual, whose responsibility [if he were *mostatee'*] is to perform the Tamattu' Hajj, was donated [the cost of] the Qiraan or Ifraad Hajj, he is not obliged to accept the offer. Similarly, if one, who had already performed the *Hajjat-al-Islam*, was offered a donation, he would not be obliged to accept the offer nor would he be obliged to the Hajj.

61. In the case of an individual who was obliged to perform the Hajj through, say, a vow and the like, but could not afford it, if he was offered a donation, he is obliged to accept it and he would be obliged to the Hajj, and through that he would discharge his duty. The same is applicable to an individual who became *mostatee'* but did not perform the Hajj until he was unable to do so, if he was offered a donation.

62. If one lost the money that was donated to him to perform the Hajj, the obligation [of the Hajj] is annulled, regardless of whether the loss occurred before, during, or after the trip, unless he has enough money to complete the Hajj, provided the Return to Sufficiency aspect is taken into account. In this case, he is obliged to perform the Hajj and this will qualify as the *Hajjat-al-Islam*.

63. In the case of Hajj by Granted, the cost of the *Had'y* should also be borne for by the donor. If the donor did not pay for the cost of the *Had'y*, the recipient would not be considered liable to the Hajj, unless he can afford the cost, in which case he would be liable to the Hajj.

64. It is permissible for the donor to withdraw his offer if he does so before the recipient declares and assumes the *ihraam*. In that case the donor should cover the cost of the journey the recipient undertook until he is back in his hometown. If the recipient declared and assumed *ihraam*, as an obligatory precaution, the donor should not withdraw his offer.

65. In the case of the donor withdrawing his offer, if the recipient had enough [money] to continue the Hajj, he would be considered *mostatee'*, and he is obliged to continue the Hajj, and this would qualify for the *Hajjat-al-Islam*. If he did not have enough money to continue the Hajj, the obligation of the Hajj is annulled for him.

66. If the recipient performed the Hajj, and afterwards it became clear that the donated money was usurped, that Hajj would not qualify for him as *Hajjat-al-Islam*. It would be the right of the owner of the money to claim his money either from the donor or from the recipient. If the owner sought the money from the recipient, [and the latter paid him,] it would be the recipient's right to refer to the donor [to recover the money he paid the owner]. Unless the recipient knew of the money being usurped, in which he has no right to refer to the donor.

67. If the recipient committed any of the *ihraam's* forbidden acts that are liable to a *kaffaarah*, he should pay for the *kaffaarah* from his own money.

68. If one made a will, vow, etc. to donate a sum of money sufficient for the Hajj, and made it conditional for it to be used for the Hajj, if the money was given to the party concerned, it would be obligatory for that individual to accept and perform the Hajj. But if the usage of the money was not made conditional for the Hajj purpose, he would neither be obliged to accept [the offer] nor to the Hajj.

69. It is *mostahab* – desirable – for one to donate money to enable those who have not performed the Hajj to do so, in which case it would qualify *Hajjat-al-Islam* for them.

Permission of the husband

70. The permission of the husband is not a condition [required] for the wife to go to the obligatory Hajj. If the wife became *mostatee'* she would be obliged to perform the Hajj, even if her husband does not give his consent, since the husband has no right to prevent her from *Hajjat-al-Islam*. However, in the case of the optional – *mostahab* – Hajj the permission of the husband is required, and he has the right to prevent her if it were to deny him the sexual rights, and if it were not, as a precaution, the same ruling applies.

71. If a woman was observing the divorce waiting period – if she was divorced a *raj'e* (Return) divorce – the rulings concerning her with respect to the obligatory and the *mostahab* Hajj are the same as those of a wife in relation to her husband, since the woman in question is still governed by the rulings of a wife.

72. The obligation of the Hajj upon a woman is not conditional on her being with a *mahram* – a male from whom she does not wear *Hijaab*. Of course it is imperative that she travels with a trustworthy individual [group].

Hajj by Vow

73. The Hajj by Vow has prerequisites of: Adolescence, Mind, Freedom, etc. as mentioned in section of Vow in the Jurisprudence texts.

74. If one vowed to visit [the shrine of] Imam Hussain *alayhis-salam* every year on the day of Arafah, and then he became *mostatee'* [in a particular year], his vow is waved in that year and he is obliged to perform the Hajj. This is applicable to any vow one may make before being *mostatee'*, and then afterwards becoming *mostatee'*, in cases when he would not be able to meet both requirements, i.e. perform the Hajj and meet the promise of the vow, the vow is waved and he is obliged to perform the Hajj.

75. If he was *mostatee'* and made a vow that contravenes the Hajj, his vow is not established and he remains obliged to the Hajj.

76. If one vowed to perform *Hajjat-al-Islam* in a year, and became *mostatee'* in that year too, or vice versa, i.e. he became *mostatee'* and

then he made that vow, in such a case one Hajj would qualify for him, declaring the *niyyah* "*Hajjat-al-Islam* that he vowed".

Hajj by Proxy

77. The prerequisites of Hajj by Proxy are: Islam, Iman, Mind, Adolescence – as a precaution, and for the agent to have no obligation to *Hajjat-al-Islam*[9]. The agency of a *Kaafir* is not valid, nor is the agency of a Muslim on behalf of a *Kaafir*. Similarly it would not be valid if the agent is insane, under aged, or if the agent is obliged to *Hajjat-al-Islam*, which has remained "established" in his responsibility[10].

78. It is imperative for the agent to know the rites of the Hajj and its rulings, even if with the help of a guide or teacher. It is also imperative that the agent is adherent to the teachings of Islam, and that the correctness and accuracy of his performance can be trusted, as a precaution, although relying on [the notion that the act of a *mu'min* is] "correct by default" is conceivable.

79. Hajj by proxy is correct whether it is done voluntarily, by hiring, by *Jo'aalah* – reward [in exchange for doing something], etc.

80. If the *mostatee'* was not able to perform the Hajj himself, he is obliged to do it by proxy, and if he could not do it by proxy, his obligation of the Hajj is annulled. However, if he remained to be liable and obliged to the Hajj until he died, it is obligatory [for his heirs] to perform it as *qadha* after his death.

81. If the *mostatee'* who is not able to perform the Hajj himself failed to do it by proxy until he died, if he had remained to be liable and obliged to the Hajj [during his life] and he had left some assets behind, it is obligatory [for his heirs to arrange] for the Hajj to be performed as *qadha*, using his assets.

---

[9] A person who is not yet *mostatee'* or has never been so, is not liable or obliged to perform *Hajjat-al-Islam*, and therefore such a person may act as an agent to perform the Hajj on behalf of someone else even if he has not discharged his own duty of the Hajj through becoming *mostatee'*.

[10] i.e. at certain stage the person became *mostatee'*, thus liable and obliged to perform the Hajj but he did not do so. He remains to be liable and obliged to Hajj regardless of his circumstances and ability in the future.

82. If it had become obligatory for an individual to perform the Hajj by proxy but he did not appoint an agent [to do so], if someone [else] offered to do it [the Hajj by proxy] for him voluntarily, that would qualify for him, although as a *mostahab* precaution he should appoint an agent [to do the Hajj by proxy] too.

83. He who was obliged for Hajj, and went to Hajj, declared and assumed the *ihraam*, and entered the precincts of the Haram, and then died before performing the rest of the rites of the Hajj, that would qualify for him as *Hajjat-al-Islam*, regardless of whether his obligation was the Tamattu', or the Qiraan, or the Ifraad. However, if he died before that, it would not qualify for him [as *Hajjat-al-Islam*], and it is imperative that it is performed as *qadha* for him. Although the qualification [of *Hajjat-al-Islam*] is conceivable if he died after [declaring and assuming] *ihraam* in general, whether or not he entered the limits of the Haram.

84. If one became *mostatee'* for the Hajj, but ignored to do so, and he did not perform the Hajj until lost his ability for the Hajj, he is obliged to perform the Hajj even if he were to go there as a rambler. If he died before performing the Hajj, it is obligatory for it to be performed as *qadha*, using the inheritance he has left, unless someone voluntarily offers to perform the Hajj on his behalf, which would qualify for him.

85. If the deceased was liable and obliged to the Hajj, [but after his death] it was doubted as to whether or not he had – [at some stage] – performed the Hajj, it should be assumed that he had acted accordingly and had performed the Hajj.

86. By merely hiring someone to perform the Hajj on behalf of the deceased does not discharge the duty of the deceased nor of his heir. It is imperative that the Hajj is performed. If it became clear that the agent, due to a reason or the lack of it, had not performed the Hajj, it is binding that a second agent is hired. The fee should be taken from the initial inheritance if it were not possible to recover it from the first agent. If the heir or the trustee were negligent, they should forfeit the fee.

87. The Hajj by proxy on behalf of a baby, a distinguishing child, or an insane is valid. In fact in the case of an individual who suffers from periodical insanity, i.e. occasionally feeling sane, and he was liable to Hajj but did not perform the Hajj – even though he was able – until he

died, it is imperative to perform the Hajj by proxy on his behalf after his death.

88. In the case of the obligatory Hajj, it is not permissible for an agent to represent two or more people [simultaneously], but it is imperative for an agent to stand-in for one person only [at any one time]. Unless the obligatory Hajj was [collectively] mandatory upon two or more people, like when two or more people vow to hire an agent [to perform] the Hajj, or if the Hajj was optional – *mostahab* – where it is permissible for one agent to represent two or more people [simultaneously].

89. It is permissible for two or more agents to perform the Hajj by proxy on behalf of one individual in the same year, regardless of whether the represented being alive or dead, or the agent being a volunteer or hired. This is applicable to the *mostahab* Hajj. It is also applicable to the obligatory Hajj, if it were multiple, and the represented individual was physically unable, or dead. Like he had vowed to perform two Hajj's, or he had vowed one Hajj but he was also liable to *Hajjat-al-Islam*, or if one of the two Hajj's was obligatory and the other *mostahab*.

90. The agent can, after completing the rites of the Hajj on behalf of the represented individual, perform the Mufradah Umrah, and the tawaaf around the House on his own behalf or on behalf of someone else.

91. It is not necessary for the agent to be male if the represented individual is a male. It is permissible for each of the man and woman to represent the other as agent. The agent performs the Hajj on behalf of the represented individual according to his/her own requirements and not according to those of the represented.

92. It is permissible to appoint the *saroorah* – i.e. the individual who has never performed Hajj before or wishes to perform the Hajj for the first time – whether male or female, to represent a male or a female individual. However, as a recommended precaution, one case should be avoided, which is the appointing of a female *saroorah* as an agent for a male *saroorah*.

93. If the deceased does not specifically stipulate that the Hajj [on his behalf] should be a *'baladi'* one, i.e. the Hajj should start from his hometown, then it is permissible to arrange for a *'miqaati'* Hajj, i.e. appoint an agent to start the Hajj from one of the *miqaat's*. The

hometown refers to the place where he normally resided, not where died, if different.

94. If the deceased had stated in his will that the Hajj to be performed on his behalf without specifying the fee, the fee should be a standard one. However, if he had specified an amount to be used for the purpose of the Hajj on his behalf, it would be imperative to act according to the request, if the amount is not more than one third [of the total inheritance] in the case of the *mostahab* Hajj. If it was more than a third, then the permission of the heir about the excess is conditional. If the deceased had specified a particular amount to be used for performing the *Hajjat-al-Islam* on his behalf, it is binding and obligatory for it to be executed, and the amount should be taken out of the total inheritance if it is not more than the minimum amount required to perform the Hajj. If it were, the excess should be taken from the third [of the total inheritance] without needing the permission of the heir.

95. If had stated in his will for a particular individual to perform the Hajj on his behalf, for a specified fee, the individual concerned is not bound by that will and he may ask for more [for a fee]. In that case another agent should be chosen to perform the Hajj. If the specified fee was more than the minimum amount required to perform the Hajj, the excess should be taken from the third [of the total inheritance] without needing the permission of the heir.

96. If the agent invalidated the Hajj, it is obligatory for him to perform its *qadha* in the following year.

97. It is not permissible for an agent to appoint another person as an agent unless he has authorised to either perform the Hajj by proxy himself or relegate it to another person, or [if he has] the specific permission of those concerned.

98. If the hire contract was general, in that it does not mention [whether] it is for him or another person [to perform the Hajj], it is required that the agent performs the Hajj, and thus it is not permitted for him to appoint someone else for the task.

99. The agent should act according to his *Marje' Taqleed* if he were a follower, or according to his *ijtihad* if he were a *mujtahid*, but not according to that of the person he is representing.

100. If the represented individual made it conditional that the agent acts according to the *fatwa* of the *Marje'* of himself [the represented], it is obligatory for the agent to act accordingly, unless [the performance of certain rites were] considered to be invalid according to his *ijtihad* or *taqleed*, in which case he should either refuse the offer, or act according to the *ihtiyaat* – precaution – that would be correct to both of them.

101. It is not permissible to appoint an agent who cannot say the *talbiyah*, or read [the Arabic texts] well, even by other's help and dictation, unless it is for a *mostahab* Hajj.

102. It is permitted for one who entered [Makkah] during the months of Hajj for performing the Mufradah Umrah, to represent someone else for the Tamattu' Hajj after finishing his Umrah. He must declare and assume *ihraam* on behalf of the one he is representing from the *miqaat* designated for the country of the individual being represented.

103. It is not permitted to perform the Mufradah Umrah by proxy after performing the Tamattu' Umrah and before performing the Hajj. Also it is not permitted to do so willingly for himself, but if he did so out of ignorance, or in disobedience, that would not harm his Hajj if it does not interfere with the two *woquf's*. The second [i.e. the Mufradah Umrah] would be considered as Tamattu' Umrah.

104. If one declared and assumed the *ihraam* for a *mostahab* Tamattu' Umrah, and after completing it, was appointed as an agent, it is not permissible for him to leave Makkah, nor to accept the agency.

105. It is mandatory for the agent to perform the task with the intention of representing the one who assigned him, even in the case of the *Tawaaf al-Nisa'*. The duty and responsibility of the individual being represented is not discharged unless the task is performed correctly and with the intention of doing so on behalf of the represented individual.

106. It is binding for the agent to act according to the conditions specified for him in terms of the type of Hajj, and its description, even in the particular route taken.

107. If the agent died after declaring and assuming the *ihraam* and entering the limits of the Haram, that qualifies for the individual being represented, and he does not need to perform another Hajj.

108. If the agent died after declaring and assuming the *ihraam* and entering the limits of the Haram, that qualifies for him and for the individual being represented, even if he had later departed the limits of the Haram. Similarly, if the agent died between [the times of] *ihraam* for the Umrah and the *ihraam* for the Hajj, that qualifies for him and the individual being represented.

109. If the agent died before [declaring and assuming] *ihraam*, or before entering the Haram with [him being in the state of] *ihraam*, they do not qualify for Hajj, taking into account some of the details of the case, although the validity is conceivable if he died after *ihraam* and before entering the Haram.

110. If one attained financial ability but without physical [ability] and he had no hope of recovering, it is obligatory for him to seek Hajj by proxy immediately.

111. If the excuse [or the reason preventing him from performing the Hajj] of the individual being represented was eliminated during the act of the agent or before starting the *ihraam*, if time was too tight, the agency is correct, and the performance of the agent qualifies for the one being represented. If, on the other hand, there was enough time, it is imperative on the individual being represented to perform the Hajj himself.

Proxy in some of the rites

112. In such cases as illness or absence, it is permissible to perform *tawaaf*, and *sa'y* by proxy, if it was not possible for the individual to do so by being helped, or carried. The same is applicable for the prayer of the *tawaaf* and *ram'y*. As for *ihraam*, *woquf*, *halq*, and the *mabeet* in Mina, doing these rites by proxy is not acceptable.

113. If a woman would not be cleansed from her menses [in time] and it would not be possible to be left behind by her group, it would be permissible for her to seek an agent to do *Tawaaf al-Nisa'* and *Tawaaf al-Ziyaarah* and their prayers on her behalf, and do the *sa'y* herself.

PART 2 – The Types of Hajj

114. There are three categories of Hajj:

1. The **Tamattu'** Hajj,
2. The **Qiraan** Hajj,
3. The **Ifraad** Hajj.

115. The Tamattu' Hajj is obligatory upon any able – *mostatee'* – adult whose hometown is at a distance of 16 *Farsakh* (88 km) or more from the Holy City of Makkah, from any direction. (Each *Farsakh* is about 5.5 km.)

116. The Qiraan and Ifraad Hajj are obligatory upon any able adult who lives at less than that distance (i.e. 88 km) from the Holy City of Makkah.

117. If one has not discharged his/her obligatory duty of the Tamattu' Hajj – also known as *Hajjat-al-Islam*, i.e. the first obligatory Hajj for those who live outside that distance, it is not sufficient for them to perform the Qiraan or the Ifraad Hajj.

118. An adult individual has the choice of performing any of these three types of Hajj, if the Hajj is a *mostahab* one, or if it is performed as a *nadhr* or vow without the type being specified, or if he has been entrusted to perform it, without specification as to which type to perform. However, the preferred choice in these cases is the Tamattu' Hajj.

119. If the adult individual was considered to have two hometowns, [i.e. permanently lived in two hometowns], one being outside the limit [of 88 km] and the other inside, he is obliged to perform [the Hajj] according to [where s/he spends] more time. So if he spent most of his time outside the limit, then he is obliged to perform the Tamattu' Hajj, otherwise the Qiraan or the Ifraad Hajj. In the case of him spending equal time between the two locations, he has the choice [of which Hajj to perform] even if he was *mostatee'* to perform one rather than the other, and the preferred choice is to perform the Tamattu' Hajj.

A brief outline of the Tamattu' Hajj

120. The Tamattu' Hajj consists of Umrah and Hajj, and a brief outline of various stage of the Hajj is as follows:

Umrah

- The individual declares and assumes the state of *ihraam* from the *miqaat* to start the *Umrah* of the Hajj.
- He travels to the holy city of Makkah, and on arrival he goes to the Grand Mosque to perform the *tawaaf* around the Ka'bah. The *tawaaf* consists of going round the Ka'bah seven times.
- He then should perform the *tawaaf* prayers – of two *rak'ah* – by Maqaam Ibrahim, or behind it.
- He should then go to perform the *sa'y* – which is to go from the mount of Safa to the mount of Marwah, and back. The *sa'y* is completed when all together seven laps have been covered between the mounts.
- At this stage one does not need to perform the *Tawaaf an-Nisa*.
- He then performs *taqseer*, which is the trimming of the hair or fingernails.
- After *taqseer*, the state of *ihraam* is lifted, and so too all restrictions and prohibitions imposed on the *muhrim* as a result of [being in] the state of *ihraam*.

Having performed and completed the Umrah, one must perform the Hajj:

Hajj

- The individual must declare and assume the state of *ihraam* in Makkah. It is preferable, or even recommended as a precaution, that this declaration is made on the day of Tarwiyah, the 8th day of Dhil-Hejjah, although it is permissible to delay this until later, such that he could ensure that he would be in [the location of] Arafaat in time for midday or noon time on the 9th day of Dhil-Hejjah.

- He should ensure that he is in Arafaat in time for midday, and that he must remain in Arafaat – *woquf* – from noontime to sunset.
- After [sunset], he should head for [the location of] Mash'ar al-Haraam. He must observe the *woquf* (remain) in Mash'ar al-Haraam between the times of *Fajr* and Sunrise.
- After sunrise he must head for [the location of] Mina in order to perform its three rituals, which are *Ram'y* (stoning of the obelisks representing Satan), *Had'y* (Sacrifice), and *Halq* (Shaving) the head (or *taqseer* where applicable).
- When he performs these rituals, it is preferable that the adult returns to Makkah on the same day, and if it was not possible, then he could go there on the following day.
- In Makkah, he must perform the *Tawaaf* of the Hajj, prays the two *rak'ah* of the *tawaaf* by the Maqaam or behind it, perform the *sa'y* as mentioned before, then performs *Tawaaf an-Nisa'* or the *Women Tawaaf*, around the Ka'bah seven times, and performs its two *rak'ah* prayers.
- It is imperative that he goes back to Mina before sunset, or [if by the time of sunset, he was still busy performing the rites of Makkah he should go back to Mina] whenever he finishes his rites, even if one third of the night has passed, in order to perform the rest of the rituals there, which is *mabeet*, [or overnight stay], in Mina during the nights of Tashreeq, and *Ram'y* [or stoning of the Jamaraat – the three obelisks or monoliths representing the Satan], during the days of Tashreeq[11].
- Having completed all these, his Hajj is complete, and s/he has discharged his duty in respect of Tamattu' Hajj.

---

[11] These are the 10th, 11th, and 12th day of Dhil-Hejjah.

Tamattu' Hajj requirements

121. A number of conditions must be observed for the Tamattu' Hajj:

a) The *niyyah* or the intention when declaring and assuming *ihraam* at the *miqaat*, when he should intend to perform the Hajj seeking nearness to Allah Almighty.

b) To perform the Hajj and the Umrah in the months of the Hajj, which are Shawwal, Dhil-Qa'dah, and Dhil-Hejjah.

c) That the Hajj and the Umrah occur in the same year.

d) Declaring and assuming *ihraam* of the Hajj – not the Umrah – from the holy city of Makkah, and it is preferable that this is made in the Grand Mosque – *Masgid al-Haraam*. If, due to any peculiar circumstances, it was not possible to do this from the holy city of Makkah, then he should do it from wherever is possible between Makkah and Arafaat. If, due to an oversight or not being conversant with the ruling, one declared the *ihraam* from elsewhere, and realised this oversight afterwards, it would be imperative for him to go back to Makkah and renew the *ihraam* from there. If it was not possible to do so, he must declare *ihraam* from where he is. However, if one deliberately declares and assumes *ihraam* from other than Makkah, his *ihraam* would be void, and it would be imperative for him to go back to Makkah and renew his *ihraam* from there, for otherwise his Hajj would be null and void.

e) The Umrah and Hajj[12] must be performed as "one-by-one", i.e. one may not hire two people to perform the Umrah and Hajj by proxy, in that one of them performs the Umrah and the other performs the Hajj. Likewise it is not permissible for one individual to volunteer to perform by proxy, the Umrah on behalf of a person, and the Hajj on behalf of another.

---

[12] The Umrah and Hajj are considered as one act, not two separate ones.

Ifraad Hajj Procedure

122. The second type of Hajj is the Ifraad Hajj, and the procedure for it is as follows:

- An adult declares and assumes *ihraam* from a *miqaat*, or from his house if it was closer to Makkah than the *miqaat*.
- He should then go to Arafaat directly and observe the *woquf* from the midday of the 9th day of Dhil-Hejjah until sunset.
- After sunset he should head towards Mash'ar al-Haraam and observe *woquf* during the period between *Fajr* and sunrise.
- After sunrise of the 10th day – the day of Eid – he should go to Mina to perform its rituals; which are *Ram'y*, the stoning, of the *Jamaraat* (the obelisks) and then *Halq* or *taqseer* – i.e. Shaving or trimming. No sacrifice is required.
- He should then go to Makkah on that day, or later, to perform the *Hajj Tawaaf* around the Ka'bah seven times, then perform the two-*rak'ah* prayers of the *tawaaf* by the *Maqaam* or behind it.
- He should then proceed to perform the *sa'y* between Safa and Marwah seven times,
- Followed by *Tawaaf an-Nisa* and its prayers.
- He should then perform the remaining rituals of Mina, the *mabeet* and *Ram'y*, which complete the Hajj.
- After this, he would also have to perform the Mufradah Umrah, where he should declare and assume *ihraam* from *"adnal-hill"*.[13] He may perform this Umrah throughout the year, although as a precaution, he should do so as soon as possible.

123. If the Ifraad Hajj was a *mostahab* one, or was due to a vow to perform an Ifraad Hajj only without an Umrah, it is sufficient for him to perform the Hajj only, and he is not required to Mufradah Umrah.

124. The conditions for the validity of the Ifraad Hajj are three:

---

[13] which literally means the nearest point where one can be without *ihraam*, in other words, the nearest point where the *ihraam* can be declared outside the Haram. For more details see case # 143.

a) the declaration of the *niyyah* or intention at the time of the *ihraam*,
b) that it is performed during the months of Hajj,
c) to declare and assume the *ihraam* from the *miqaat* or from his house.

125. If one declares and assumes the *ihraam* with the intention of performing a *mostahab* Ifraad Hajj, it would not be valid for him to change his intention to perform the Mufradah Umrah in order to perform the Tamattu' Hajj on behalf of someone else.

Qiraan Hajj Procedure

The third category of Hajj is the Qiraan Hajj, and the procedure for it is as follows:

The procedure for the Qiraan Hajj is exactly the same as that for Ifraad, with the exception that in this case the person performing this Hajj must have the sacrificial animal accompany him at the time of *ihraam*, [and it should accompany him until the time of slaughter] whereas in the case of Ifraad he does not need to offer a sacrifice.

The person who performs this Hajj has the option of uttering the *talbiyah*, or marking the animal with a sign or a collar.

Tamattu' Hajj Details

127. The Tamattu' Hajj consists of two acts of worship:

1. The Tamattu' Umrah
2. The Tamattu' Hajj

The Rites of the Tamattu' Umrah

128. The Umrah of Tamattu' consists of five rites:

1. *Ihraam*.
2. *Tawaaf* around the Holy Ka'bah seven cycles.
3. *Salaat al-Tawaaf* or the *tawaaf* prayer of two *rak'ah* by Maqaam Ibrahim or behind it.
4. *Sa'y* between the Safa and Marwah seven times.
5. *Taqseer* or trimming of some of one's hair or fingernails.

129. In the Umrah of Tamattu' the declaration of the *niyyah* or intention is obligatory, and so too is to perform the Umrah and Hajj together during the months of Hajj, which are Shawwaal, Dhil-Qa'dah, and Dhil-Hejjah in the same year, as mentioned previously.

130. The *niyyah* in the Umrah of Tamattu' – or in any other act of worship – is the mental intention, and the person intends in his heart that, "I perform the Hajj of Tamattu', beginning with the Umrah of Tamattu', whilst seeking nearness to Allah Almighty". It is recommended to verbally utter the intention in all rites of Hajj and Umrah.

1. IHRAAM

131. The first of the rites of Umrah of Tamattu' is *ihraam*, and it is obligatory for the *ihraam* to take place in one of the designated locations known as the *miqaat*.

The various Miqaat's

132. It is obligatory to declare and assume the *ihraam* at one of the designated *miqaat's*. The locations of the various *miqaat's* have been specified by Rasulollah *salla-llahu-alayhi-wa-aalih* for the people (coming from the) various countries, directions and horizons. It is not permitted for the *Haajj* – the person performing the Hajj – to cross the limits, the *miqaat*, unless one has declared and assumed *ihraam* from one of the *miqaat's* or from their proximity. The various *miqaat* locations are as follows:

1. Masgid al-Shajarah
2. Waadi al-Aqiq
3. al-Juhfah
4. Qern al-Manaazel
5. Yalamlam
6. *adnal-hill*
7. The house of the pilgrim if it was closest to Makkah than any of the other *miqaat* locations.

[See case # 145 for the special case of using Jeddah airport as a "*miqaat*" location.]

133. The *miqaat* of **Masgid al-Shajarah** (The Tree Mosque) is also known as Dhul-Hulayfah, and it is the *miqaat* for the people of the holy city of Medina or those from other countries who pass from the city.

134. Masgid al-Shajarah is the furthest *miqaat* from the holy city of Makkah, and it is about seven km outside the holy city of Medina. Thus it is not permissible for one to cross Masgid al-Shajarah without *ihraam*. Also it is not permissible to postpone the *ihraam* until al-Juhfah, unless it is for exceptional circumstances such as illness or weakness, etc. However, if one chooses an alternative route that does not pass through the location of the Masgid al-Shajarah, or even through the proximity of it at any stage, then it is permissible for him to postpone the *ihraam* until the al-Juhfah *miqaat*, or any other *miqaat*. But if one were at the proximity of Masgid al-Shajarah, then he is not allowed to leave location

of the proximity (of the *miqaat*) except by declaring and assuming *ihraam*.

135. The legal definition of proximity here is that if one stands facing the [direction] of the sacred Ka'bah, the *miqaat* would be on his right or left, without being too far from him.

136. One who is in a state of *Janaabah*[14] or (a woman) who is experiencing *haydh* – the monthly menstruation period – may not enter the Masgid al-Shajarah and declare and assume *ihraam* from it, unless they are passing through it without stopping, such that they enter one door and leave from another, when they can declare and assume the *ihraam* and say the *talbiyah* en route as they pass through the mosque. If it was not possible to pass through, it is obligatory for them to declare and assume the *ihraam* from outside the mosque, but closely adjacent to it, with the mosque being either on their left or right, as a precaution.

137. Declaring and assuming *ihraam* under the ceiling of the Masgid al-Shajarah is not considered sheltering. [Generally sheltering is prohibited for a muhrim when on the move.]

138. It is permitted to declare and assume *ihraam* in the extension to the Masgid al-Shajarah, as there is no difference between the old building and the new. The same is applicable to other *miqaat's*.

139. **Wadi al-Aqiq**, is the second of the *miqaat's*, and is about 100 km from the holy city of Makkah. This *miqaat* is for the people of Iraq and Najd and those people coming through this route to Makkah. The beginning location of this *miqaat* in the direction of Iraq is known as al-Maslakh, and the mid location is known as Ghamrah, and the ending location of this *miqaat* is known as Thaat-Erq.

---

[14] A person is in the state of *Janaabah* whenever s/he engages in penetrative sexual intercourse, or (in the case of men) whenever ejaculation of semen occurs even without the any sexual intercourse.

140. **al-Juhfah** is the *miqaat* for the people of the Shaam and Egypt. It is also the *miqaat* for those people coming from other countries through their route, if they do not pass by another *miqaat*, or if they passed by the other *miqaat* without declaring and assuming the *ihraam*, and it is not possible for them to go back to declare the *ihraam*. In this case it is incumbent on them to declare and assume *ihraam* from al-Juhfah.

141. **Qern al-Manaazel** is about 94 km from Makkah, and it is the *miqaat* for the people of Ta'ef, and those coming from their direction.

142. **Yalamlam** is a mountain from the mountain series of Tahamah, and is also some 94 km from Makkah. It is the *miqaat* for the people of Yemen, and those coming from their direction to Makkah.

143. *adnal-hill*,[15] is the limit/border of the Haram. [The Haram encompasses the holy city of Makkah from all sides, and it is an area of about 500 square kilometres approximately.] This limit is the *miqaat* for those who do not come to Makkah by crossing any of the above five *miqaat's* or their not too distant proximities, while not being able to go to other *miqaat's*.

144. He whose house is closer to Makkah than the *miqaat's*, then his house is his *miqaat*.

145. The *Haajj* (pilgrim) who arrives at Jeddah by airplane, and wishes to go to Makkah [directly], may declare and assume *ihraam* from Jeddah by making a [prior] *nadhr* (vow), by saying "I make it my duty to Allah to declare and assume *ihraam* from Jeddah." As for declaring and assuming *ihraam* in the aircraft while it is flying in the proximity (of a *miqaat*), it is not normally achievable.

146. If one failed to declare and assume the *ihraam* from one of the designated *miqaat's*, due to reasons of not knowing, or forgetting the mandatory nature of *ihraam* from the *miqaat*, or if he did not know that

---

[15] literally meaning "the nearest point one can be without *ihraam*", in other words, the nearest point *ihraam* can be declared outside the Haram.

this was the actual place of the *miqaat* – provided he was not *moqassir*[16] in his forgetting or not knowing, as a precaution – or if he did not intend to perform the rites nor entering Makkah, and therefore passed through the *miqaat* with that purpose, and afterwards he decided to enter Makkah or perform the rites, as a precaution, it is mandatory for him to go back to the particular *miqaat* if it is possible, even if there is another *miqaat* ahead of him. However if it is not possible for him to go back to the first *miqaat*, it is incumbent on him to declare and assume *ihraam* from the *miqaat* ahead of him. If there is no *miqaat* ahead of him, he should then declare and assume *ihraam* from where he is. However, if he had entered the Haram he must go back to the borders of the Haram, and declare and assume the *ihraam* outside the Haram if it was possible, and if it was not possible in anyway to go back [to the borders of the Haram], he must declare and assume the *ihraam* from where he is, and his Umrah is valid.

147. If one forgot to declare and assume the *ihraam* until he performed all the obligatory (rites), his Umrah is valid. So too, if he did not declare and assume *ihraam* because he did not know it was mandatory for him to do so, or if he assumed *ihraam* from a place other than the proximity of a *miqaat* thinking that it was [the proximity], and other such reasons, in all such cases his Umrah is valid, provided, as a precaution, this is due to him being a *qaasir*[17] not *moqassir* [in his failure to learn and understand the issues concerned].

---

[16] *Moqassir* means one who does not know the ruling regarding certain aspect (of a religious duty) and he is aware of this ignorance or shortcoming and where to find the answer for, e.g. through certain books, references, or individuals with the appropriate expertise, but does not make the effort to seek the answer. In this way he has failed to discharge his duty. For comparison also see *qaasir*.

[17] *Qaasir* means one who does not know the ruling of a certain aspect of a religious duty, but in fact he is not aware of this ignorance and naturally does not seek the answer to the case concerned since he believes that what he is doing is correct. Thus one should not assume that what he is doing is always correct, and ensure to check with reference books or expert individuals. As a matter of fact it is imperative and obligatory for the individual to learn and know all aspects that s/he may come across in the course of one's life concerning the relevant issues.

148. If one deliberately did not perform the *ihraam*, and then it became impossible or impractical for him to go back to the particular *miqaat* to perform the *ihraam*, in this case there are three scenarios to consider:

    a)   If he intended to enter Makkah only, without meaning to perform the (Hajj) rites, in this case he has committed a sin by not performing the *ihraam*, and by entering Makkah without it, and generally there is not need for *qadha'* – i.e. no need to perform the *ihraam* later on.

    b)   If he had decided to do the Mufradah Umrah, it is sufficient to perform the *ihraam* from *adnal-hill*, even though he has committed a sin by crossing the *miqaat* without an *ihraam*.

    c)   If he had decided to perform the Hajj, then he must perform the *ihraam* in a similar way to the case of the one who had forgotten to do it, as described previously. He must go back to the *miqaat* [that he came from] if it were possible to do so, and perform the *ihraam* there, even if there is another *miqaat* en route. If this was not possible, then he should go to the *miqaat* en route, [i.e. the nearest *miqaat*], and his Hajj is valid.

149. If one performs the *ihraam* before arriving at the *miqaat,* without having made any legal vow, his case is the same as the one who has not performed the *ihraam*, and therefore it is not allowed for him to enter the Haram and perform the rites, until he performs the correct procedure as mentioned earlier. He must renew his *ihraam* from the *miqaat* by renewing his *niyyah*, and the *talbiyah*, etc. as it is required at the declaration and assuming of *ihraam* from a *miqaat*.

150. It is not allowed for an adult to enter the holy city of Makkah, and not even to enter the Haram with intention of entering Makkah, unless with a valid *ihraam* observing all the required conditions from the (appropriate) *miqaat*. As for entering the Haram without the intention of entering Makkah, [he does not have to assume *ihraam*, although] it is preferable to observe precaution by performing it [before entering the Haram, in which case he would have to go to Makkah to do the Mufradah Umrah, and thus be released from the ihraam].

151. If the adult needed to enter and leave the holy city of Makkah frequently because of his job, then such an individual may enter Makkah without *ihraam*.

152. It is also permissible to enter Makkah without *ihraam* for one who had originally entered it with a valid *ihraam* observing all the required conditions, then left it, and then return to the city within the month in which he had performed the *ihraam*. However, if one month after his *ihraam* he wishes to enter Makkah, he must perform a new *ihraam* from the *miqaat*.

153. It is important to note that the references made to the month in this respect do not suggest lunar months, but the criterion is the passage of thirty days.

The Mandatory Steps of the *IHRAAM*

154. The mandatory steps of the *ihraam* are:

1. Wearing the two garments of *ihraam*
2. The intention, or *niyyah*.
3. The *talbiyah*.

1. Wearing the two garments of the *ihraam*

155. After removing the clothing that is not permitted to wear, the two pieces of garments for *ihraam* must be worn. One of the garments is worn round the waist to cover the body from navel level to the knees, and the other should be used for covering the shoulders at least. As a precaution, it is required that a woman wears the two pieces of garments of *ihraam* on top of her clothing, and performs the *talbiyah*, even though it is permissible for her to remove the two garments afterwards.

156. It is conditional, as an obligatory precaution, that the garment worn around the waist is not thin, revealing the skin, and so too for the garment covering the shoulders. It is also conditional for the *ihraam* garments:

- to be of such material that is valid for the daily obligatory prayers for men,
- not to be *nagis* with which one may not be able to perform the daily prayers,
- not to be made from products of an animal the meat of which is not permissible for (Muslim) consumption,
- not to be usurped, nor any gold is allowed to be used in it,
- not to be made from silk even for women,
- as a precaution, not to be made from leather, even if taken from animals whose meat is permissible to eat,
- as a precaution, to be woven or textile such as towels, and not matted or compressed.

157. If one or both of the *ihraam* garments were made *nagis*, then as a precaution the *muhrim* – the individual in the state of *ihraam* must either replace the *nagis* garment or wash it to make *taahir* immediately. If he does not do that he has sinned but his *ihraam* is valid. However, if part of the body became *nagis*, it is not incumbent on him to make it *taahir* immediately, even though may be is as a precaution.

158. If there was a wound on the body of the *muhrim* and there was blood on the dressing / plaster, and it was not possible for him to remove the dressing when time was short, the rulings of *Jabirah* applies to him. [you will find the details in this respect in *risalah* of Islamic laws.]

159. It is not mandatory for the *muhrim* to continually wear the *ihraam* garments; for the *muhrim* may change them or take them off completely, like when going to the bathroom or having a shower. This applies to both genders.

160. It is not mandatory to be *taahir*, like after going to the toilet, when declaring *ihraam*. Thus one who is in the state of *Janaabah*, or a *Ha'edh* [a woman who is experiencing the *haydh* – the monthly menses], or one who does not have *wudhu* may declare and assume *ihraam*. However, if one wanted to perform the *ihraam* prayers, the prayers would not be valid unless [being *taahir* and] with *wudhu*.

161. If due to oversight or ignorance of the ruling, one wore the *ihraam* garments without removing his normal clothing, then whenever he remembered or realised the ruling of the case, must remove his normal clothing, and his *ihraam* is valid. The same is also applicable if an individual, after declaring and assuming *ihraam,* wears his normal clothing, either having forgotten or due to ignorance of the case.

162. There is no objection to wearing more than the normal set of *ihraam* garment, whether at the time of declaring *ihraam* or afterwards, to protect oneself against the weather.

2. *Niyyah*

163. Declaration of *niyyah* or intention is mandatory for *ihraam*. It is the resolution of performing *ihraam*, seeking nearness to Allah Almighty. The meaning of *ihraam* is to abstain from and relinquish a number of things, details of which will be given later.

164. In an exception to other acts of worship, it is recommended that the *niyyah* is verbally uttered in this case. After removing all sewn clothing, and wearing the two *ihraam* garments, one should say, *"I declare and assume the ihraam for the Umrah of TAMATTU' for Hajjat-al-Islam seeking nearness to Allah Almighty".*

3. *Talbiyah*

165. Without *talbiyah*, *ihraam* would not be established, (although) in the case of Qiraan Hajj, the *ihraam* is established with *talbiyah*, or marking the animal with a sign or a collar.

166. The obligatory *talbiyah*[18] takes the following form of reciting [the four phrases]:

---

[18] *Talbiyah* literally means compliance, fulfilment, or carrying out the orders of Allah Almighty.

Labbayk Allahumma Labbayk.   I heed to your call O Lord, I heed.

Labbayka Laa Shareeka Laka   I heed that (O You) You have no
Labbayk.   partner, I heed.

In Nal-Hamda,   Truly, All the Praise,
Wan Ne'mata,   and the Bliss,
Laka Wal Mulk.   are Yours and the Sovereignty is
    too.

Laa Shareeka Laka Labbayk.   There is no partner of Yours, I heed.
The last word may be added as a recommended
precaution.

167. It is obligatory that the *talbiyah* is recited at least once, and with it the *ihraam* is established. Of course it is *mostahab* that the Haajj (pilgrim) repeat it when he wakes up, after each of the daily obligatory prayers, when getting on a vehicle, or going up or down a hill, etc. It is also recommended to repeat it during the night (Sahar), even if the *muhrim* was in the state of *Janaabah* or *Haydh*. In the case of Umrah it is recommended that he does not stop it until he can see the houses of the city of Makkah, when he should stop. In the case of the Hajj, it is recommended that one does not stop it until midday of the Day of Arafah – the 9th day of Dhil-Hejjah – when should stop.

168. It is obligatory to recite the *talbiyah* in the correct Arabic pronunciation. It is not sufficient to pronounce it with a variant accent or pronunciation if one can recite it correctly. If one cannot recite it correctly, someone else should help him to recite it by dictating to him. If there was no such person, he should recite whatever he can, and as a *mostahab* precaution, he should pronounce it with the variant accent together with reciting the translation (of the *talbiyah*) as well as getting an agent to recite the *talbiyah* on his behalf, after he had done it himself.

169. A dumb must perform the *talbiyah* by making gestures with his fingers, and moving his tongue at the same time.

170. It is not mandatory to perform the *talbiyah* immediately when the two *ihraam* garments are worn and the *niyyah* stated, even though it is as a precaution. If one says it after a [short] delay, his *ihraam* is valid.

171. If the Haajj (pilgrim) forgot to say the *talbiyah* at the place of the *ihraam*, which is the *miqaat*, and remembered the oversight after crossing the *miqaat*, it is obligatory for him to go back to the *miqaat* to perform it. If it was not possible for him to go back, he should say it where he is. If, after entering the Haram, the factor preventing him from going back was eliminated, then he must leave the Haram, if possible, and perform the *talbiyah*, otherwise, he should do so where he is. If he had committed one of the forbidden acts of *ihraam* before saying the *talbiyah*, he is not liable to a *kaffaarah* – compensation – even if had crossed the *miqaat*.

172. If he doubted whether the *talbiyah* he had done is correct or not, he should presume that it is correct. If he doubted whether he did perform the *talbiyah* or not, and he had not crossed the *miqaat*, he should presume that he had not, and it is obligatory for him to perform the *talbiyah* then. If he had done one of the forbidden acts of the *ihraam* that demands a *kaffaarah*, and he doubted whether he did that act after the *talbiyah* or before it, he is not liable to *kaffaarah*.

The haraam *things and acts of* ihraam

173. The *muhrim*, i.e. one who is in the state of *ihraam*, must refrain from 25 issues:

1. Hunting land animals,
2. Sexual intercourse (with one's spouse),
3. Pleasure seeking with one' spouse,
4. Performing marriage contract or witnessing it,
5. Masturbation,
6. Perfume,
7. Wearing sewn clothing (applicable only to men),
8. Wearing slippers, shoes, or socks,
9. Using *Kohl* powder on the eyes,
10. Looking in the mirror,
11. *Fosuq*, which is lying, swearing, and boasting,
12. *Jidaal*, which is to enter into arguments, disputes, or Quarrelling,
13. Killing insects found on humans [such as lice],
14. Beautification,
15. Applying oil,
16. Removing hair (from the body),
17. (Using) Henna,
18. Covering the head (in the case of men),
19. For a woman to cover her face,
20. Sheltering in shade, for men,
21. Causing bleeding,
22. Clipping the finger nails,
23. Pulling a tooth,
24. Wearing arms/weapons,
25. Uprooting a tree or any vegetation of the Haram.

1. Hunting land animals

174. It is forbidden for a *muhrim* – one who is in the state of *ihraam* – to hunt a land [/air] animal, excluding other animals. It is also forbidden to catch the animal, or help in its hunt, even by guiding (the hunter) or

pointing (to it) or encaging it, or any other means in the hunt process. It is also forbidden to slaughter the animal or eat from its meat.

175. It is permissible to kill savage predatory animals if the *muhrim* feared them. It is also permissible for non-*muhrim* to kill birds of prey if they hurt the pigeons of the Haram, however, the *muhrim*, as a precaution, should abstain from killing them.

176. If he hunted a game or slaughtered it, (it would count as) *meetah* – dead animal meat – and thus it is forbidden for him or anyone else to eat from it, and one may not perform the prayers wearing the leather made from its skin.

177. It is prohibited to hunt a land animal, but a sea animal is not prohibited to hunt. By sea animal it is meant those animals that live, reproduce and grow in water, even in little streams of water. Also it is not prohibited to slaughter a tame animal, even if had turned wild.

178. The ruling of the young is the same as its parent, and so too is that of the egg. As for lotus, it is classified as a land animal, and therefore it may not be hunted, and it is forbidden to eat.

179. If there was a doubt as to whether the animal is of land or sea, it is not mandatory to avoid it.

180. Just as it is forbidden for a *muhrim* to hunt even outside the Haram, it is also forbidden for a non-*muhrim* to hunt within the boundaries of the Haram, and he is liable to a *kaffaarah* just as a *muhrim* is, although the *kaffaarah* may sometimes differ. If a *muhrim* killed an animal within the boundaries of the Haram, he is liable to the cost of the animal as well as the *kaffaarah*.

Kaffaarah of hunting

181. The following *kaffaaraat* [compensations, penalties] are obligatory in hunting:

- Hunting an Ostrich is liable to the *kaffaarah* of a camel.
- Hunting a wild cow is liable to the *kaffaarah* of a tame cow.
- Hunting a Zebra is liable to the *kaffaarah* of a camel or a tame cow.
- Hunting a deer, a rabbit, or a fox is liable to the *kaffaarah* of a sheep.

182. If one hunted [an animal] that is liable to a camel, but was unable to find a camel, he should– with the cost of a camel – buy wheat and divide it between the poor. However, it would be sufficient to give food to sixty poor people, each receiving one *modd* of wheat. Each *modd* is equivalent to approximately 750 grams. If he was unable to give that, he should fast for 18 days instead. The fasting does not need to be consecutive, and he can fast a few days at a time if he wished.

183. If one hunted [an animal] that is liable to a tame cow, but was unable to find a cow, he should buy wheat – with the cost of a cow – and divide it between the poor. However, it would be sufficient to give food to thirty poor people, each receiving one *modd* of wheat. If he was unable to give that, he should fast for 9 days instead.

184. If one hunted [an animal] that is liable to a sheep, but was unable to find one, he should give food to ten poor people, each receiving one *modd* of wheat. If he was unable to give that, he should fast for 3 days instead.

185. If the *muhrim* hunted a pigeon or a similar bird, and slaughtered it, he must compensate for this by [offering] a sheep. If he broke a pigeon egg and the like, and there was a chick inside that had life, he is liable to [offering] a sheep, and if the chick was motionless, he is liable to the cost of the egg, which he should give to charity.

186. If a non-*muhrim* caught and killed a pigeon or other similar bird within the boundaries of the Haram, then he is liable to either give one

Dirham[19] to the poor, or give him the cost of the bird, although the second option is preferable as a precaution.

187. If he hunted a sand grouse, partridge, and such like, he is liable to a sheep.[20]

188. If he hunted a sparrow, wren, skylark, and the like outside [the limit of] the Haram, he has the option of giving either the cost of the kill or a *modd* of wheat to charity. If he was inside the Haram, his liability is twice, and so too if he hunted a young. If he broke its egg, he should give the cost of it to charity.

189. If he killed a lotus, he has the option of giving a handful of wheat or one date to charity, but if he hunted a lot of lotuses, he is liable to *kaffaarah* of a sheep. If there were many lotuses on the road, it is incumbent on the *muhrim* to choose an alternative route. If this was not possible, and some of the lotuses died as a result of him stepping over them, he is not liable to anything.

190. If he killed a lizard, he is liable to a handful of wheat, and if he unintentionally killed a wasp he is liable to some[21] wheat, but if he killed it to repel its harm, there is no liability [to a *kaffaarah*].

191. If a group took part in the hunt, every one of them is liable to a separate *kaffaarah*.

---

[19] A Dirham is equivalent to 0.3153 gram of gold, which is almost one-hundredth of an ounce, i.e. if an ounce of gold is $350, then a Dirham is equivalent to $3.50.

[20] It is prohibited for a non-*muhrim* to hunt within the boundaries of the Haram, just as it is so for a *muhrim* to hunt outside the boundaries of the Haram. In both cases they are liable to *kaffaarah* as seen from the examples given in the cases here. Needless to say it is prohibited for a *muhrim* to hunt within the boundaries of the Haram.

[21] This could be less than a handful.

192. The *kaffaarah* of eating the game is the same as the hunt itself. So if a *muhrim* hunted a game and ate it, he is liable to two *kaffaarah's*; one for hunting, and another for eating from it.

193. If one was accompanied by a game, it is obligatory for him to release it when he enters [the limits of] the Haram, and if he did not release it until it died, he is liable to its *kaffaarah*. Also if someone had hunted an animal when he was not in the state of *ihraam*, and then declared and assumed *ihraam*, he must release the game even if he has not entered the Haram.

194. Liability to killing or eating the game is mandatory regardless of whether this was deliberate or by negligence, oversight, or ignorance of the ruling of the case.

2. Sexual intercourse

195. Sexual intercourse is absolutely forbidden for a *muhrim*, whether one was in a state of *ihraam* for Hajj or for Umrah.

196. Women are forbidden for *muhrim* men, just as men are forbidden for *muhrim* women.

The *kaffaarah* for sexual intercourse

197. One who is in the state of *ihraam* for the Umrah of Tamattu', if he had finished the *sa'y*, but had not done the *taqseer*, and knowingly and deliberately committed sexual intercourse with his spouse, he is liable to *kaffaarah* of a camel. If he could not afford it, he should offer a cow, and failing that he must offer a sheep, and his Umrah is valid. If, on the other hand, he committed this before performing the *sa'y* he is liable to the *kaffaarah* and his Umrah is invalidated, and it is obligatory for him to repeat the Umrah if possible.

198. If one had declared and assumed the *ihraam* for the Hajj, and before the *woquf* in the Mash'ar al-Haraam, he knowingly and deliberately committed sexual intercourse with his spouse, if the woman had willingly

agreed to it too; the Hajj of both is invalidated. However, they are both obliged to complete the Hajj, and repeat the Hajj in the second year, regardless of whether their Hajj was obligatory or optional (*mostahab*). If the woman had not willingly agreed to it, her Hajj is not invalidated, and the man must pay two *kaffaarah*, and the woman is not obliged to anything. Furthermore, it is mandatory to part between the man and woman from where this act was committed during this Hajj, and during the second Hajj until they arrive in the same stage again.[22]

199. If a *muhrim* for Hajj knowingly and deliberately engages in sexual intercourse with his spouse after the *woquf* in Mash'ar al-Haraam and before performing *Tawaaf an-Nisa'*, he is obliged to offer a *kaffaarah* but his Hajj is not invalidated. If he committed this act after three-and-a-half cycles of *Tawaaf-an-Nisa'*, his Hajj is valid, but as a recommended precaution, he should give the *kaffaarah*. If he did this after the completion of *tawaaf-an-Nisa'* and before the prayers of this *tawaaf*, his Hajj is valid and he is not obliged to give *kaffaarah*.

200. If a *muhrim* for the Mufradah Umrah knowingly and deliberately engages in sexual intercourse with his spouse before the *sa'y*, he is obliged to offer a *kaffaarah* and his Umrah is invalidated. However, he must complete this Umrah, and then perform a new *ihraam* for the Mufradah Umrah, and perform all its rites.

201. If a *muhrim* for the Mufradah Umrah knowingly and deliberately engages in sexual intercourse with his spouse after *Tawaaf-an-Nisa'* and before the prayers of the *tawaaf*, he is not obliged to a *kaffaarah* and his Umrah is valid. If this was at a time when the *Tawaaf-an-Nisa'* was

---

[22] During the current Hajj, this separation must last until the end of the Hajj. Because he engaged in sexual intercourse with his wife, he must also observe the *mabeet* in Mina on the eve of the 13th and also perform the *Ram'y* of the three Jamaraat on the 13th day of Dhil-Hejjah. If he had performed the rites of Makkah – the two *tawaafs* and the *sa'y* – prior to day 13, then that would be the end of the Hajj, and if not, the end of Hajj would be when he completes the rites of Makkah. As for the separation between the couple on the next Hajj, it starts from the moment of the declaration of the ihraam for the Hajj until they arrive at the same stage where they committed the act last year.

partially done, his Hajj is not invalidated, but as a recommended precaution, he should give a *kaffaarah*.

202. If a *muhrim* woman willingly consents to sexual intercourse, the rulings in her case are the same as those of a man in terms of obligation of the *kaffaarah*, invalidation of the Hajj, etc.

203. If a *muhrim* man engages in sexual intercourse with his spouse while not being conversant with the ruling of the case, or due to negligence and oversight, regardless of whether this negligence and oversight was in respect of the rulings of the case or in [him being] in the state of *ihraam*, his Hajj and Umrah are not invalidated, and he is not obliged to give *kaffaarah*.

3. Seeking pleasure

204. It is forbidden to seek pleasure from one's spouse by say kissing, looking, touching, etc. if this was with passion and lust. However, if the touching and looking was without passion or lust, then it is not objectionable. Also hugging is not objectionable if it is not with the intention of pleasure. As for kissing it should be absolutely avoided, as a precaution.

205. All of this is applicable to woman, just as it is for man, and therefore it is not permitted for her to seek pleasure by looking at her husband or touch him with lust or passion, or kiss him.

206. If a *muhrim* knowingly and deliberately, lustfully kissed his wife, and as a result ejaculated, he is obliged to give a *kaffaarah* of a camel, and the same is applicable even if he did not ejaculate. If he did not do that out of lust, and he ejaculated, he is obliged to give a *kaffaarah* of a sheep, and if he did not ejaculate he should give a *kaffaarah* of a sheep as an obligatory precaution.

207. If a *muhrim* lustfully touched his wife, and as a result, he ejaculated, he is obliged to give a *kaffaarah* of camel.

208. If the *muhrim* lustfully fondled his wife or looked at her, such that as a result he ejaculated, he is obliged to give a *kaffaarah* of a camel.

209. If a *muhrim* knowingly and deliberately looked at a non-*mahram* woman, and as a result ejaculated, regardless of whether it was with or without lust, and regardless of whether or not he had intended the ejaculation, he is obliged to give a *kaffaarah* of a camel, if he was well off, otherwise he should give a *kaffaarah* of a cow, or if he was poor he should give a *kaffaarah* of a sheep. However, if he did not ejaculate he is not liable to a *kaffaarah*, although by this act he had committed disobedience and sinned.

4. Performing a marriage contract or witnessing it

210. It is forbidden for a *muhrim* to perform a marriage contract, whether this is for himself or for others, and regardless of it being a permanent, temporary, or proxy marriage, and whether the persons involved were *muhrim* or non-*muhrim*. It is also forbidden if someone else performed a marriage contract for him as his agent, even if agency was given to the agent prior to him assuming the state of *ihraam*.

211. As a precaution, one should also abstain from seeking permission of marriage [from the father or guardian of the girl] even if his intentions are to conclude the marriage contract after the *ihraam*. As for the *return* in the case of a divorce, there is no objection to it if it is done during the state of *ihraam*.

212. It is forbidden for a *muhrim* to attend a marriage contract ceremony, or witness a marriage contract even for someone else. This is applicable even if the other party was not in the state of *ihraam*. Also it is forbidden for him to act as witness, even if he agreed to do so when he was not in the state of *ihraam*.

213. If a *muhrim* conducted the marriage contract for a couple who were both *muhrim*, and the couple had sexual intercourse, if this was done knowingly and deliberately, for all concerned, every one of them must give a *kaffaarah* of a camel, and the marriage contract is invalid, and the

wife is forever forbidden *(haraam)* for the husband, [i.e. the husband can never marry that woman again in the future]. This is in addition to the rulings on sexual intercourse [concerning a *muhrim*] as mentioned previously. One is not liable to *kaffaarah* if this was due to ignorance of the ruling, negligence, oversight, or compulsion.[23]

214. If a *muhrim* married a *muhrimah* [a female *muhrim*] by conducting the marriage contract himself, then the same rulings as above apply, in terms of knowledge and ignorance, etc.

215. If a *muhrim* performed the marriage contract for a couple who were both not in the state of *ihraam*, the marriage contract is invalid, and the man who performed the marriage contract must give a *kaffaarah* of a camel.

5. Masturbation

216. Masturbation, which is seeking to ejaculate by means of hand or any other means, is forbidden [in general], and it is also one of the forbidden acts of *ihraam*.

217. If a *muhrim* masturbated using his hands, his ruling is that of a *muhrim* who had sexual intercourse with his wife; in terms of the invalidity [of his rituals] and the obligation of completing [the rest of the rituals]. He must repeat it the same year if he was *muhrim* for the Mufradah Umrah, and in the following year if he was *muhrim* for the Hajj, etc.

218. If a *muhrim* did not masturbate by his hands, but only by looking at a woman [who is not his wife], or by imagination, he is obliged to give a *kaffaarah* of a camel if he is well off, a cow if he is considered average, or a sheep if he is not well off. In this case his Hajj is not invalidated if he was *muhrim* for Hajj, nor is his Umrah if he was *muhrim* for Umrah.

---

[23] The only difference between these two scenarios is the non-liability to *kaffaarah* in the latter category, otherwise under all circumstances the marriage is invalid and the couple may never marry again.

6. Perfume

219. It is forbidden for a *muhrim* to use perfume, such as Musk, *Anber*, *Warce*, saffron, etc. in all it types and applications, and as precaution all kinds of perfume and fragrant should be avoided.

220. If a *muhrim* was compelled to perfume, he must block his nose. He must also do so if he bought it from the perfume seller, or sat next to an individual who was wearing perfume, etc.

221. If any perfume fell on his garments, or on his body, he must remove it immediately by washing etc.

222. There is no objection in eating flowers and herbs, fruits, medicine, etc. that are not normally considered as perfume, even if they had pleasant fragrant. The ultimate precaution in this case would be not to smell them.

223. It is not permissible for a *muhrim* to block his nose when he comes across bad smells.

224. The *kaffaarah* for using saffron, musk, *anber*, and *warce* whether smelling them or using them for eating or wearing, is a sheep. There is no *kaffaarah* for other kinds of perfume.

7. Wearing sewn clothing for men

225. It is forbidden for male *muhrims* to wear sewn clothing, such as shirt, trousers, coat, cloak, or clothing with buttons or sleeves, etc. even if they were not sewn. It is also forbidden to wear shields, armour, or the *malbad* – worn by shepherds. All of these are forbidden for a *muhrim* unless compelled to do so, in which case it is permissible to do so, and as a precaution, should give a *kaffaarah* of a sheep. The restrictions mentioned here are not applicable to women.

226. It is not permissible for male *muhrim* to tie as a knot his *ihraam*, but there is no objection to prick the ends together using a pin and such like.

227. It is permissible for a *muhrim* to wear the following things, even though they are sewn:

1.   the *hemyaan*, a wide belt with built in pockets, to keep cash, valuables, etc.
2.   belt,
3.   hernia belt if needed, and it is permissible to tie it as a knot, as well as knotting the belt and *hemyaan* if he wore one,
4.   shoes, if they do not cover the top surface of the feet, although as a precaution one should refrain [from wearing them].

228. It is permissible for women to wear sewn clothing in general. The exception is that women are not allowed to wear gloves.

229. If a male *muhrim* wears sewn clothing knowingly and deliberately, he is liable to the *kaffaarah* of a sheep.

8. Wearing slippers and socks

230. It is forbidden for the male *muhrim* to wear boots, slippers, socks, etc. that cover the feet. If he cannot find the Arabic slippers, it is permitted for him to wear those footwear that cover the feet provided, as a precaution, he tears off the front of the shoes such that feet are not covered.

231. It is permitted for women to wear socks and such like, and as a *mostahab* precaution, [part of the] socks should be torn to prevent covering the feet.

232. Polystyrene flippers that are not sewn and do not cover the feet are ideal for *ihraam*, and it is not necessary for them to be white coloured, any colour is permissible.

233. There is no objection to the feet being covered by the *ihraam* garments, etc. when walking, sitting, or during sleep.

234. The *kaffaarah* for wearing socks or slippers is a sheep if this was done out of choice. If he wore any of these, by tearing the front to reveal the feet, then there is no liability to *kaffaarah*.

9. Wearing *kohl* eyeliner

235. It is forbidden for a *muhrim* [male or female] to wear black *kohl* eyeliner [make up for the eyes], even if one does not intend for beautification. As a precaution, wearing any kind of black *kohl* eyeliner should be avoided even if not intended for beautification. Wearing non-black eyeliners is permissible if it is not intended for beautification.

236. If one wore *kohl*, there is no *kaffaarah* to give, other than *istighfaar,* seeking forgiveness from Allah Almighty. It is recommended – *mostahab* – that he gives *kaffaarah* of a sheep.

10. Looking into mirrors

237. It is forbidden for a *muhrim* to look in a mirror for the purpose of beautification / dressing up. If by doing so he does not seek beautification, like car driver looking in the mirror to watch what is behind him, then there is no objection to that.

238. There is no objection to looking in clear water, and any other liquid or glass screen on cars that reflect the [image of the] body. Also there is no object to wearing spectacles if it is not intended for beautification or adornment.

239. If a *muhrim* looked in a mirror for the purpose of dressing up, he is not liable to a *kaffaarah*, except *istighfaar* – seeking forgiveness from Allah Almighty – although it is recommended that he should then renew the *talbiyah*. See case # 166 for the declaration of *talbiyah*.

11. *Fosuq*

240. It is forbidden to commit *Fosuq*, which is attributing lies, whether to Allah Almighty, the prophet *salla-llahu-alayhi-wa-aalih*, the *Ma'soom*

Imams *alayhum-as-salam*, or the people in general. So too is using swearwords, boasting about himself, humiliating and demeaning others, or using foul language.

241. The *kaffaarah* of *fosuq* if *istighfaar* – seeking forgiveness from Allah Almighty, and his *ihraam* is not invalidated.

12. Arguing

242. It is forbidden for a *muhrim* to engage in arguments, which is to swear by Allah – saying *"la wallah"* or *"bala wallah"* meaning "by Allah, No!" or "by Allah, Yes!" This is the case – i.e. forbidden – even in the absence of quarrelling, as a precaution. However, it is permissible to do so if it is [absolutely] necessary to prove the truth, or repel falsehood, or if it is to glorify [Allah, Rasulollah, and the Ahl-ul-Bayt] or show loyalty [to them].

243. If, in the course of an argument, one swore twice on an issue and he was saying the truth, then he has committed a sin, and he is not obliged to give a *kaffaarah* except *istighfaar*, and if he swore three times or more, he is obliged to give a *kaffaarah* of a sheep.

244. If, in the course of an argument, one swore once on an issue and he was lying, he is obliged to a *kaffaarah* of a sheep, and if he swore twice on a lie, he is obliged to *kaffaarah* of a cow, and if he swore three times on a lie, he is obliged to *kaffaarah* of a camel.

13. Killing of insects found on the body

245. It is forbidden for a *muhrim* to kill the insects found on [his] body, such as lice, and as a precaution there is no difference between the processes in which they are killed, whether directly or indirectly, by means of [chemical] substance, or throwing it so that it would be prone to be killed. As a precaution, the same is applicable for moving the insect from one place to another such that it would be prone to fall off. If however, the insect does not form on one's body, such as a flea or tick, then it is permissible to kill it. The tick may not be moved from the body

of the camel, but it is permissible to move it from the body of the human or kill it.

246. It is permissible to kill insects such as bug or flea, and such likes in the process of protecting oneself, although as a *mostahab* precaution one should avoid this, especially in the Haram.

247. In the case of killing the insects found on the body, or throwing them off the body, the *kaffaarah* is a handful of food to give as charity to the poor.

14. Beautification

248. It is forbidden for *muhrim* to engage in any act that constitutes beautification or adornment, such as wearing a ring. It is permissible to wear a *khatam* if it is intended as a *Sunnah*.

249. It is forbidden for a woman in the state of *ihraam* to wear jewellery for the purpose of beautification, although what she normally or habitually wears before *ihraam* is not objectionable provided that it is not visible.

250. There is no objection to wearing a watch in the state of *ihraam* if it is not intended for the purpose of adornment or beautification.

251. The *kaffaarah* for beautification is a sheep, as a precaution, and no *kaffaarah* is applicable for wearing *khatam*.

15. Applying oil

252. It is forbidden for a *muhrim* to use oil to apply to the body, or other body lotions, even if they do not have any scent or perfume. However, it is permissible if it was for a necessity or treatment.

253. There is no *kaffaarah* for applying oil to the body except *istighfaar*, however, if this was deliberate, and out of choice and knowledge, it is recommended that a *kaffaarah* of a sheep is given.

16. Hair removal

254. It is forbidden for a *muhrim* to remove any hair from his/her body or from someone else's, even few strands of hair. The exception here is if there was a necessity such as [if the head of the person was] lice-ridden, severe headache [that could be eased by shaving the head], or if there was an annoying hair strand in the eye. In these cases hair removal is permissible, and it is obligatory to give a *kaffaarah*. There is no liability to a *kaffaarah* if one removed someone else's hair, although it is not permissible for him to do so [to begin with] even if the other person is not in the state of *ihraam*.

255. It is permissible for a *muhrim* to scratch his body, provided he takes care the hair is not removed because of the scratching.

256. There is no objection if some hair unintentionally falls in the process of *wudhu* or *Ghusl*, when one normally runs his fingers through the hair, as necessary. However, if this went beyond the norm, then it would be objectionable, and as a precaution one should give a *kaffaarah* of two handfuls of food.

257. If, because of a necessity, a *muhrim* shaves his head, he is liable to *kaffaarah* of a sheep, or three days' fasting, or feeding six poor people the amount of two *modd* of wheat each. Also if he shaved his head without a necessity, he has the choice between them, although it is recommended, as a precaution, to give a *kaffaarah* of a sheep.

258. If a *muhrim* shaved other than his head, knowingly and deliberately, whether the shaving is permitted outside *ihraam* or not – such as shaving the beard – as a precaution his *kaffaarah* is a sheep.

17. Henna

259. The use of Henna during *ihraam* is forbidden as a precaution, and it is preferable to avoid it (Henna) before *ihraam*, if any traces still remain at the time of *ihraam*. It is preferable to avoid anything that contradicts the *muhrim* to be dishevelled and dust-covered.

18. Covering the head – for men

260. It is forbidden for a male *muhrim* to cover his head, which is defined as the hair growing area and the ears. The prohibition applies whether the head is covered fully or partially, and regardless of the kind of cover used; if it touches the head, even mud or henna. Also it is not permitted for him to submerge in water or in any other liquid, or to carry anything on the head, if it meant that it covers the head, as a precaution.

261. It is permitted to cover the head with part of the body such as the hand, and also it is permitted to wipe the hand on the head when performing *wudhu*, or when pouring water over the head during *Ghusl*, etc. as this is not regarded as covering [the head].

262. It is permitted for a *muhrim* to sleep even if this constitutes part of his head being covered due to its contact with the ground [or pillow]. It is also permitted for him to pour water over his head or stand below the showerhead for [the purpose of] washing, etc. it is also permitted for him to scratch his head if he was sure that any hair would not fall [as a result].

263. If due to lapse and oversight he covered his head, he is not liable to anything, but must remove the cover as soon as he realises his oversight.

264. The *kaffaarah* of covering the head is a sheep, and a *kaffaarah* is liable each time the head is covered.

19. Women face covering

265. While in the state of *ihraam*, it is forbidden for a woman to cover her face with the cover [she normally wears] such that it touches her face, even when asleep.

266. It is permitted for female *muhrim* to sleep even if this constitutes part of her face being covered by coming in contact with the ground or [the pillow]. It is also permitted for her to cover her face with a veil such that it is distant from her face. It is permitted for her to cover her face with hands. It is also permitted for her to wear her *aba*, and cover her

face provided the face cover is kept away from her face. It is also permitted if part of her face [i.e. he forehead] is covered, if this is in aid of covering the head as required for the daily obligatory prayers.

267. The *kaffaarah* for a woman covering her face is a sheep.

20. Sheltering in shade – for men

268. It is forbidden for a male *muhrim* to seek shelter in the shade while on the move, whether on foot or during a ride, like using an umbrella or riding in a roofed vehicle. As a *mostahab* precaution, he should avoid seeking shelter on either side of his body, even though it is permissible to walk in the shadow of a vehicle or anything provided that it would not be over his head, and it is permissible to use one's bare hands as a protection from the sun.

269. On the basis of what can be derived from the *hadith*, there is no distinguishing between day and night in so far as the prohibition of the seeking shelter is concerned, thus it is not permissible to seek shelter during the night.

270. It is permissible for a *muhrim*, while on the move, to pass underneath a bridge or go through a tunnel, and it is permissible to declare and assume *ihraam* under the roof of Masgid al-Shajarah, as mentioned earlier.

271. It is permissible for a *muhrim* to seek shelter under a roof, if he stopped his journey for a rest between the *miqaat* and Makkah, like going to the motorway restaurants, or if he needed to go to offices to organise his travel schedule, etc. and as a recommended precaution, he should avoid using umbrella.

272. It is permissible to seek shelter from the sun even with an umbrella once in the holy city of Makkah, and there is no difference in this respect between old and new Makkah. This is also applicable once in Arafaat and Mina, and if one who is in Mina, wished to go to the slaughter place or to the *Jamaraat*.

273. It is permissible for one who declares and assumes *ihraam* from the mosque of al-Tan'eem mosque for the Mufradah Umrah to ride a roofed car, for these days the mosque in question is considered to be inside the holy city of Makkah.

274. It is permissible to seek shelter in necessity, like when it is extremely hot or cold, or when it is raining – if it is likely to harm him, but he must give *kaffaarah*.

275. In general sheltering is permissible for women and children, with no liability to *kaffaarah*.

276. A male guide for the women pilgrims who needs to be with them, he is permitted to ride a roofed vehicle with them, so too is the driver who fears for his car if he left it, and in both of these cases, they [the guide and car driver] are liable to *kaffaarah*.

277. If no cars are available for the pilgrim other than the roofed cars, or if he cannot ride cars but the roofed ones – due to an illness say – then it is permitted for him to ride the roofed ones, but he is liable to a *kaffaarah*.

278. The narrow crossbars of roofless cars do not provide shelter, [and therefore the shade that they produce does not constitute shelter].

279. Whenever he was compelled to seek shelter, he is liable to a *kaffaarah*, and during one *ihraam*, it is sufficient to give one *kaffaarah* for more than one occasion of shelter seeking. However, as a *mostahab* precaution, he should give a separate *kaffaarah* for each day.

280. The *kaffaarah* for seeking shelter is a sheep, and it is permitted for him to slaughter it in his home country.

21. Causing bleeding

281. It is forbidden for a *muhrim* to cause [any part of] his body to bleed, by any means, whether by venesection, or *hijamah* (cupping or

bloodletting), or while brushing the teeth, or scratching, etc. unless it is for a necessity. Some of the circumstances of necessity are itchy skin disorders that are associated with scratching, cutting open and squeezing a boil or sore, if leaving them unattended by not scratching or cutting them would hurt him.

282. The *kaffaarah* for causing bleeding unnecessarily is a sheep, and if he were compelled, he would not be liable to a *kaffaarah*.

22. Clipping fingernails

283. Fingernail clipping is forbidden for a *muhrim* even if it is to clip one fingernail, or part of, unless [the particular fingernail] is hurting him, for example if part of the nail was broken, or if the finger needed to be treated, and this required the nail to be clipped.

284. The *kaffaarah* for clipping each fingernail is one *modd* of food, and that for all of one's fingers only a sheep, and so too for one's toes only. If the clipping of all fingers and toes was done in one session, then the *kaffaarah* is one sheep, but if the fingernails were clipped in one session, and the toenails in another, then the *kaffaarah* is two sheep. All of this is applicable if it was done knowingly and deliberately.

23. Pulling a tooth

285. It is forbidden for a *muhrim* to pull a tooth if it were to bleed, and the *kaffaarah* is a sheep, however, if one was compelled to do so, it is permissible and one is not liable to a *kaffaarah*.

24. Wearing of arms

286. It is forbidden for *muhrim* to wear arms, such as sword, dagger, pistol, rifle, and such like that is considered a weapon, and one who is carrying it is considered armed. However, if one is not considered armed, such as carrying a small knife that a pilgrim might need for his personal use, then there is no objection to it. As a precaution, a weapon must not be carried overtly even if it is not being worn.

287. The *kaffaarah* for wearing arms out of choice is a sheep as a *mostahab* precaution.

25. Uprooting the plants of the Haram

288. It is forbidden for a *muhrim* to cut or uproot anything that grows in the Haram, whether or not s/he was in the state of *ihraam*, or s/he was performing Hajj or Umrah, etc.

289. The exceptions from the above ruling are:

- *al-Edhkher* (lemon grass), which is a famous herb,
- date palm,
- fruit trees,
- anything that one has planted himself,
- the plant that had grown in his house or property, if it grew after moving in.

290. The *kaffaarah* for uprooting a large tree is a cow, and for a small tree is a sheep, and if it was part of the tree, [then the *kaffaarah*] is the price of that [part], and that for grass is *istighfaar*. All of this is applicable if it was done knowingly and deliberately. However, if it was done in ignorance, or due to oversight etc. then one is not liable to anything.

Miscellaneous

291. Whatever *kaffaarah* becomes obligatory for him during the *ihraam* of Umrah, he should slaughter in Makkah, and whatever *kaffaarah* becomes obligatory for him during the *ihraam* of Hajj, he should slaughter in Mina, and give it to the poor of the faithful, or send it to their representative(s). If this was not possible, since there were no destitute, nor their representative, in that case one has the choice of slaughtering in Makkah / Mina or doing so back in his homeland and distributing it between the poor and needy.

292. If one committed an act, which is liable to a *kaffaarah* while ignorant of the ruling, then he is not liable to a *kaffaarah*. The same is applicable if this was due to an oversight, except in hunting. As for hunting, the *kaffaarah* is applicable if an act requiring it was committed, regardless of this being in ignorance, oversight or deliberate.

293. If one of the forbidden acts of *ihraam* occurred coercively, then the *muhrim* is not liable to anything, such as when someone else forcefully sheltered him, or covered his head.

294. In every case when he was liable to a sheep, he could if he wished offer a goat instead.

Limits of the Haram

295. The Haram encompasses the holy city of Makkah from all sides, and it is an area of about 500 square kilometres.

2. TAWAAF

296. The second rite of the Tamattu' Umrah is *tawaaf*, and the *tawaaf* is also compulsory in the Tamattu' Hajj, the Qiraan and Ifraad Hajj as well as the Ifraad Umrah that is also known as the Mufradah Umrah.

297. This *tawaaf* is a *Rukn* or a principal element, and therefore the Hajj or Umrah is invalidated if it is deliberately abandoned, contrary to the case of *tawaaf al-Nisa'*.

298. If one deliberately abandons the *tawaaf*, and as a result is not able to perform it before the *woquf* in Arafaat, his Umrah is thus invalidated and his Hajj is reverted to Ifraad. He must therefore keep his state of *ihraam*, and directly head to Arafaat. He should observe the *woquf* there and perform all the rites of the Hajj, as it will be given later *InSha'Allah*. He should then perform the Mufradah Umrah after finishing the Hajj.

299. The same ruling applies to the *moqassir*, one who was ignorant [of the ruling] due to negligence as the one who deliberately [abandoned to

perform the *tawaaf*] as a precaution. As a priority precaution, the same also applies to the *qaasir,* one who did not know the rulings. However, this does not apply to the one who forgot to perform the *tawaaf*, for he should perform the *tawaaf* of the Umrah as soon as he remembers it, even if he remembered this after performing the Hajj rites, and when Dhil-Hejjah had ended. In that case he should also repeat the *sa'y*, as a precaution. This is applicable if he was still in Makkah, but if he remembered that he had not performed the *tawaaf* after he had left the holy city, if he had arrived at his hometown, he should assign someone to perform the *tawaaf* on his behalf if it is practically difficult for him to go back to Makkah. If however, he had not arrived at his hometown, he should go back to Makkah to perform the *tawaaf* himself if it is not too difficult to go back. If it proved too difficult to do so, he should then appoint someone to do the *tawaaf* on his behalf, even the following year if necessary. Similarly, the *sa'y* should be repeated, either by himself or, failing that, by proxy, as a precaution.

300. If one performed the *tawaaf* incorrectly, his Umrah is invalidated if it was for Umrah, or his Hajj is invalidated if he was performing the Hajj, regardless of whether he was *moqassir* as a precaution, or *qaasir* as a priority precaution.

301. If an ill or disable person cannot perform the *tawaaf* on his own, if he can seek help from others, say by leaning on them or being carried by them, then he is obliged to do so. If however, he was in a state that he could not even do so, then he should appoint an agent to do the *tawaaf* on his behalf.

302. If a woman experienced *haydh* – the monthly menstruation period, or *nifaas* – the blood due to postpartum or childbirth, it is obligatory for her to wait until the start time of the *woquf* in Arafaat. If she was *taahir* [i.e. the end of *haydh* or *nifaas*] before the designated time of the *woquf*, such that she could perform the *tawaaf* [and its two-*rak'ah* prayer, the *sa'y* and the *taqseer*] in time for the *woquf* in Arafaat, then she is obliged to do so. If she was not *taahir* before the Designated time of *woquf*, it is permissible for her to perform the *sa'y* and the *taqseer* [only], so that she would cease to be in the state of *ihraam* of the Tamattu' Umrah. She

should then declare and assume the *ihraam* of the Hajj. She must perform the *tawaaf* for the Tamattu' Umrah, and the two-*rak'ah* prayer of the *tawaaf* once she is *taahir* [She should do them after performing the rites of Makkah, which are the two *tawaafs* and the *sa'y*].

Alternatively, it is permissible for her to revert her Hajj [from the Tamattu' Umrah] to the Ifraad Hajj [without renewing her *ihraam*], go to Arafaat, while in the state of menses, and observe the *woquf* there, and after sunset head to Mash'ar al-Haraam, and then from there she goes to Mina on the Day of Eid, and perform all the rites as described. After this [the completion of the Ifraad Hajj] she must perform the Mufradah Umrah, as will be described later *InSha'Allah*.

303. If a woman knows that she would not be *taahir* until the end of the day of Arafah, she must either declare and assume the state of *ihraam* for the Ifraad Hajj to begin with, or alternatively she must declare and assume the *ihraam* for the Tamattu' Umrah, perform the *sa'y* and *taqseer*[24], thereby releasing herself from the *ihraam*, and starts the Hajj [by declaring and assuming the *ihraam* for the Hajj and proceed as normal]. She must perform, as *qadha*, the *tawaaf* of the Tamattu' Umrah, and its two-*rak'ah* prayer after she is *taahir*.

Conditions and requirements of *tawaaf*

304. A number of conditions must be met in *tawaaf*:

1. *Tahaarah* from faeces and urine,
2. *Tahaarah* cleanliness of the body and clothing,
3. Circumcision (for male),
4. the covering of *awrah*
5. the legality of the clothing/garments
6. the *niyyah* or intention.

1. Cleanliness

---

[24] Because she is not *taahir*, she may not perform the *tawaaf* and its prayer, as it is normally required.

305. It is conditional in *tawaaf*, that one is clean and *taahir* from faeces and urine, if the *tawaaf* is an obligatory one. If the *tawaaf* was *mostahab*, *tahaarah* from urine is not conditional. It is forbidden for one who is not *taahir* from faeces to enter Masgid al-Haraam – the Grand Mosque – and *tawaaf* can only be done in the Masgid al-Haraam, around the sacred Ka'bah.

306. One who is not able to achieve *tahaarah* by washing with water, due to an illness and such likes, *tahaarah* by earth – *tayammum* – can replace the *tahaarah* by water. Thus, if one, due to a reason, could not wash after excretion, he must perform *tayammum* instead. With the exception of *Janaabah*, he is also required to perform *wudhu* if he could do the *wudhu*, otherwise he would need to do another *tayammum* instead of the *wudhu*, and then perform the *tawaaf*.

307. In the case of a woman experiencing *Istihaadha* – undue or lesser menses [this is compared with the normal monthly menses referred to as *Haydh*], if it is not possible for her to achieve *tahaarah* by washing with water, then it is sufficient for her to perform the emergency *tahaarah* – i.e. the *tayammum* – and by doing so her *tawaaf* is valid. Similarly, the same ruling applies to other cases such as those with difficulties in controlling their bowel/wind movement or urine, although it is a priority precaution to do the *tawaaf* himself, and then hire an agent to do so on his behalf.

308. If one performed the *tawaaf*, and afterwards remembered that he did not have *tahaarah*, if the *tawaaf* was obligatory, it is mandatory for him to seek *tahaarah* and repeat the *tawaaf* again.

309. If in the course of the *tawaaf*, one passes wind, urine, etc. [which annuls the *wudhu*, and any such occurrence is referred to as *hadath*] if he had not exceeded half of the *tawaaf*, then he must seek *tahaarah* [and/or *wudhu*] and repeat the *tawaaf* again from the beginning. If on the other hand, this occurred when he had exceeded half of the *tawaaf*, then he must seek *tahaarah* [and/or *wudhu*] and complete the *tawaaf* from where the *hadath* occurred. In this case, both the first and this latter part of *tawaaf* are valid.

310. If one had doubt between being in a state of *tahaarah* and the occurrence of *hadath*, regardless of whether this [doubt] was before, after or during the *tawaaf*, the same ruling applies as that of the daily obligatory prayers. If he had a doubt about the occurrence of the *hadath* after being sure of being in the state of *tahaarah* [e.g. *wudhu*], then he should assume being in the state of *tahaarah*, and his *tawaaf* is valid. If however, he doubted [being] in the state of *tahaarah*, after being sure about the occurrence of the *hadath*, then he must seek *tahaarah* and it is not valid for him to perform *tawaaf* without being in the state of *tahaarah*. On the other hand, if he doubted being in the state of *tahaarah*, and this doubt arose after the completion of the *tawaaf*, he should ignore the doubt, and his *tawaaf* is valid.

311. If in the course of performing the *tawaaf* one realised being in the state of *Janaabah* or going through the monthly menses, s/he must abort the *tawaaf* and leave the Masgid al-Haraam immediately.

2. Cleanliness of the body and clothing

312. It is obligatory upon anyone who wishes to perform the *tawaaf* to cleans and make *taahir* his body and clothing from anything *nagis*, except that which is disregarded for *salaat*, the daily obligatory prayers, such as a blood spot that is less than a coin, or the blood excreted from boils or sores. It is [in fact] a *mostahab* precaution to clean and purify even the disregarded *nagis* thing that is permitted in *salaat*. If it proved too difficult to avoid [these latter ones], for example one could not avoid the boil or sore blood, then there is no objection to his *tawaaf*.

313. If one performed the *tawaaf*, and after finishing it he realised his body or clothing was *nagis*, his *tawaaf* is valid.

314. If in the course of performing the *tawaaf* one realised there is a *nagis* [thing] on his body or clothing, if he could remove it without disrupting, violating or contradicting the *tawaaf* [process] then he must do so, and continue his *tawaaf* after removing it. Similarly if he came into contact with a *nagis* thing while performing the *tawaaf*, he must remove it and continue his *tawaaf*.

73

315. If he was not able to remove the *nagis* thing from his body or clothing while doing the *tawaaf*, he must [stop the *tawaaf*] cleans the relevant part, and perform the *tawaaf* again if he had done less than three-and-a-half rounds of *tawaaf*, while if he had reached that stage [or more], he must resume his *tawaaf* from the point he stopped for *tahaarah*.

316. If he forgot that there was something *nagis* on his body or clothing, and performed the *tawaaf* with it, but remembered it after completing the *tawaaf*, his *tawaaf* is valid.

3. Circumcision

317. One of the requirements of *tawaaf* is circumcision – for the male, but not for the female [pilgrims]. It is a requirement for the male child to be circumcised too, if he is not so by birth, for the *tawaaf* is not valid without circumcision.

4. Covering of *Awrah*

318. Another requirement of *tawaaf* is the covering of the *Awrah* [which includes the private parts] as mentioned in the requirements of *salaat*. A *tawaaf* is not valid if it is done while one is bare, even if one was sure that there is no one who could see him.

5. Legality of the clothing

319. Legality of the clothing worn by the pilgrim is another requirement for the validity of *tawaaf*, i.e. it must not be usurped. If one performed *tawaaf* while wearing usurped clothing, his *tawaaf* is null and void.

6. *Niyyah* or intention

320. Another requirement of *tawaaf* is *niyyah*, that he declares the *niyyah* or intention to perform the *tawaaf* in compliance with the orders of Allah Almighty. He should state, "I perform the *tawaaf* around this House, seven rounds for the Tamattu' Umrah, seeking nearness to Allah Almighty".

321. The above six requirements are applicable to all obligatory *tawaaf* of any kind, whether the *tawaaf* is for *al-Ziyaarah* or *al-Nisa' tawaaf*, or for the Tamattu' Umrah or Hajj, or for the Ifraad or Qiraan Hajj, or for the Mufradah Umrah.

Obligations of *Tawaaf*

322. The obligations of *tawaaf* are:

1. to begin and end the *tawaaf* with the Hajar al-Aswad,
2. the House should be on the left hand side [of the Haajj],
3. Hijr Isma'el should be within the [circular route of] *tawaaf*,
4. to keep clear of the House,
5. [the circular route of] the *tawaaf* should be between the House and Maqaam Ibrahim, as a precaution, if it is not too much of a problem,
6. the number of rounds [of the *tawaaf*],
7. continuity,

1. To begin and end with Hajar al-Aswad

323. It is not correct to begin the *tawaaf* from other than Hajar al-Aswad nor is it to end it at other than the Hajar al-Aswad.

324. For establishing the correct beginning and ending with the Hajar al-Aswad, it is sufficient to be generally in line with it when beginning a cycle or ending one, and it is not necessary to be very precise about the first part of the body being in line with the first part of the Hajar.

325. If one stood in line with the Hajar al-Aswad, with the Hajar on his left hand side, and [began] the first cycle of the *tawaaf*, and went round the Ka'bah until he reached the Hajar al-Aswad again, this round trip constitute as one cycle around the Ka'bah, the like of which one must perform seven cycles in total, and it is not necessary for one to do more than that.

2. To make the House to be on his left hand side

326. The *tawaaf* would not be correct if one does not allow the Ka'bah to be on his left hand side, if one does the opposite, i.e. to allow the Ka'bah to be on his right hand side [when performing the *tawaaf*], his *tawaaf* would be null and void.[25]

327. It is sufficient for the House to be on his left in general, as accepted by common perception, and it is not necessary for him to watch the minarets [as an aid to keep in line], and slight deviation does not invalidate it [the *tawaaf*].

328. [In the process of the tawaaf,] if the House turned out to be on his right hand side, or he faced it, or if his back was to the House, even for one step – deliberately or by oversight – that step, or any more than that, would not be correct, and he is obliged to repeat the steps that were taken in the incorrect position or direction if it is possible for him to do so as necessary, and nothing prevents him from this attempt, and if something did prevent him, it would be preferable for him to do as much as he can. However, if due to overcrowding he was deviated slightly for one or two steps, such that his left shoulder was not in the direction of the House, it is unlikely that this would be objectionable.

3. Including Hijr Isma'el

329. It is obligatory to include Hijr Isma'el inside the [circular route of] *tawaaf*. Hijr Isma'el is the burial place of the prophet Isma'el, his mother Haajer, and a number of other prophets peace be upon them.

330. It is obligatory to make Hijr Isma'el on his left, for if one performed the *tawaaf* by going between it and the House, by making the House on his left and the Hijr on his right, that would invalidate his *tawaaf* and he must repeat that cycle only.

4. Keeping clear of the House

---

[25] i.e. the *tawaaf* must be performed in an anticlockwise manner around the Ka'bah, and not clockwise.

331. The *tawaaf* is not correct if it is done inside the House. However, if one performed the *tawaaf* on the wall of the Hijr or on the shadhrawaan of the Ka'bah, which are the remaining section of the foundation of the old building after the new building was erected, the *tawaaf* would be correct. There is no objection if one touched the wall of the House or the Hijr with his [left] hand [in the process of the *tawaaf*].

332. If he performed part of the *tawaaf* incorrectly, he is obliged to amend and rectify the incorrect part, if he was not excused, say through ignorance by being *moqassir*, but if he was excused, say through ignorance by being *qaasir*, it would be preferable for him to do so.

5. Performing the *tawaaf* between the House and Maqaam Ibrahim

333. As a precaution, and without undue difficulty, one should not include Maqaam Ibrahim inside the circular route of the *tawaaf*, but leave the Maqaam on his right and the House on his left, and the *tawaaf* path in between, observing a distance from all sides [of the House], which is estimated to be around 30 feet approximately.

334. It is permitted to perform the *tawaaf* around the sacred Ka'bah at a distance greater than 30 feet if it proved difficult to meet that requirement. It is also permitted to perform the *tawaaf* on the first floor of Masgid al-Haraam, or on the second floor (the roof level) of the Masgid if it was too difficult to do so on the ground floor, and the *tawaaf* around the Ka'bah would be correct, like when there is a great mass of pilgrims performing the *tawaaf*.

6. The number of rounds [of the *tawaaf*]

335. It is obligatory that the number of cycles of the *tawaaf* around the sacred Ka'bah is seven rounds, [beginning] from the Hajar al-Aswad and [ending] at the Hajar al-Aswad, nothing more or less.

336. If one adds to or deducts from the *tawaaf* at its beginning or during the course of the *tawaaf*, as a precaution the *tawaaf* would be invalidated in all respects.

337. If the addition was a small amount, before the start of the *tawaaf*, then there is no objection to it if it was in preparation for the *tawaaf*.

338. After completing the seven laps of the *tawaaf*, if by oversight there was an increase of less than one complete cycle around the Ka'bah, it is mandatory to abort the extra cycle, but if this increase was one complete cycle or more, as a precaution, he should complete the *tawaaf*, i.e. by performing another six laps so that a *tawaaf* of seven laps is completed. The second *tawaaf* would be regarded as *nafilah* (extra). He should perform the prayer for the first *tawaaf* before the *sa'y*, and perform the prayer for the second *tawaaf* after the *sa'y*.

7. Continuity in *tawaaf*

339. Continuity is a requirement in the obligatory *tawaaf*, which means that one should perform the laps of the *tawaaf* continually and not to do anything between the *tawaaf* cycles that would contradict that continuity in the obligatory *tawaaf*. Continuity is not a requirement in the *mostahab tawaaf*.

340. If some rounds were missed or corrupted from the *tawaaf*, but he was still in the process of *tawaaf*, he should then complete the *tawaaf* by performing the required rounds.   By doing so he would have satisfactorily completed the *tawaaf*, regardless of whether the corruption was deliberate or due to an oversight, or whether this was before reaching the halfway stage or after, or whether the *tawaaf* was obligatory or *mostahab*.

341. If some rounds were missed or corrupted from the *tawaaf* and he engaged in an act that contravened the continuity [of the *tawaaf*], if the *tawaaf* was an optional one, he should complete the *tawaaf*, and it is considered valid. If the *tawaaf* was obligatory, and the corruption was due to an oversight and not deliberate, if he had completed four rounds, on the basis of this [four rounds] he should perform the missed or corrupted round(s) as soon as he remembered this. If he had not done four rounds, he should restart the *tawaaf* again.

342. If he forgot to do some rounds of the *tawaaf*, and did not remember the failure until after leaving Makkah, and it is not possible for him to return [to Makkah], he should appoint someone to perform the missing rounds on his behalf if he had done at least four rounds of *tawaaf*, or the entire *tawaaf* if he had not done [four rounds].

343. If one doubted the [number of rounds of] *tawaaf*, his *tawaaf* is invalidated and should restart the *tawaaf* anew, regardless of whether the doubt

- arose by the *Rukn* or before,
- or [it was about being] six or seven rounds [have been accomplished],
- or five and six rounds or less than that,
- or whether there has been any addition or not.

As a precaution he must complete the *tawaaf* based on the minimum [number of rounds], and then restart the *tawaaf*.

If the *tawaaf* was an *mostahab* one – *nafilah* – he should complete the *tawaaf* based on the minimum [number of rounds] and he does not need to restart [the *tawaaf*].

344. If he doubted the number of rounds he had done after [finishing] the *tawaaf*, or if he doubted their correctness, and this doubt arose after he finished his *tawaaf*, he should ignore that doubt, assuming the correctness of his *tawaaf*. Similarly if at the end of the seventh round he doubted if this was the seventh or eighth round or more, the doubt is void, and his *tawaaf* is correct.

345. As far as the *tawaaf* is concerned, the ruling of uncertainty [concerning any aspects of *tawaaf*] is the same as that of doubt.[26]

---

[26] meaning that if you give the probability that the *tawaaf* round you are doing is the fourth and not the fifth, but you are not certain of this, you should treat this uncertainty as a doubt, and thus one should act accordingly.

346. In the case of doubt, it is permitted to confirm the number of rounds done by relying on two aspects; 1) testimony of two just witnesses, or 2) trust of a reliable and truthful individual, a single individual would be sufficient, with no distinction between the individual being a man, woman, or child, nor being a committed Muslim or not.

347. If he doubted [the number of rounds he has done] during the *tawaaf*, and then started a new *tawaaf*, and during the new *tawaaf* remembered the number of rounds of the first *tawaaf*, if the first *tawaaf* was complete, then he aborts the new one, and if it was incomplete, he should perform the necessary rounds to complete the *tawaaf*, and it is not necessary for him to complete the new *tawaaf*.

348. If while performing the payer of the *tawaaf*, he realized that he had not completed the *tawaaf*, he [should] abort his prayer, and complete his *tawaaf*, regardless of whether he had exceeded the halfway stage of the *tawaaf* or not, or whether he had started the prayer due to ignorance, oversight or forgetfulness. However, if he realized this after the prayer [of the *tawaaf*], he must complete the *tawaaf*, and as a precaution repeat the prayer [of the *tawaaf*].

349. If he started the *sa'y* and then realized that he had not completed the *tawaaf*, he should abort the *sa'y* and return to complete his *tawaaf*, even if the remainder of his *tawaaf* was more than half. He should repeat the prayer of the *tawaaf* as a precaution. He should then return to complete his *sa'y* even if the remainder of his *sa'y* was more than half. However, it is *mostahab* – recommended – for him to perform the *tawaaf* and *sa'y* anew.

350. If during the *tawaaf*, it was time for the obligatory prayers, it is recommended for him to stop the *tawaaf*, even if he had not reached the halfway stage, perform the obligatory prayers, and then go back to complete the *tawaaf*.

3. Prayer of the *tawaaf*

351. The third rite of the Tamattu' Umrah is *Salaat al-tawaaf* or the *tawaaf* Prayer. The prayer should be performed by or behind Maqaam Ibrahim peace by upon him, which is a rock on which is the footprint of the prophet Ibrahim peace be upon him. The prayer can be performed behind the Maqaam up to the furthest point of the Mosque, as it is commonly accepted. The prayer is of two *rak'ah*, just like the *Fajr* prayer, and one has the option of reading it silently or audibly. As a precaution the prayer should be performed after the *tawaaf* immediately, as accepted by common definition.

352. The performance of the prayer [of *tawaaf*] is to be by the Maqaam on either side, or behind it up to the furthest point of the Mosque, and if this was not possible, he could perform the prayer anywhere in Masgid al-Haraam he wished. This is for the case of obligatory *tawaaf*. However, in the case of an initially *mostahab tawaaf*, he has the option of performing prayer [of the *tawaaf*] anywhere in the Mosque he wished, in general, i.e. whether or not he is compelled, [e.g. due to overcrowding], although as a *mostahab* precaution he should do so only when compelled.

353. The *nagis* things that are disregarded for the obligatory prayers, are also ignored for the *tawaaf* prayer.

354. If one forgot to perform the prayer of the *tawaaf*, it is obligatory upon him to do so whenever he remembers it. It is not mandatory for him to perform the Sa 'y again. This is applicable if he was still in Makkah. If however, he did not remember it until he left Makkah, he should perform it wherever he remembers, although it is recommended that he returns [to Makkah] to perform it by the Maqaam, if this does not constitute hardship for him. If the person dies before performing the prayer, it is obligatory upon his *wali*: oldest son/heir to perform it, just like all of his other prayers.

355. If one deliberately abandons the *tawaaf* prayer, the rest of the rites that he is liable to are correct, and remains liable to performing that prayer, like the one who had forgotten to do so.

356. It is permitted to perform the *tawaaf* prayer in congregation (*Jamaa'ah*). If he wished to perform two *tawaaf's*, he should perform the prayer after each *tawaaf*, and it is discouraged – *makruh* – to perform two *tawaaf's* consecutively and then perform two prayers for the two *tawaaf's*.

Some of the issues concerning women

357. If the monthly menstruation bleeding starts before performing the *tawaaf* prayer or during the *tawaaf*, if she had done completed four rounds or more she should abort the *tawaaf* and /or prayer and leave the Mosque immediately. She could perform the rest of rites in terms of the *sa'y* and *taqseer* if [these rites] were for the Umrah. She should wait until she is *taahir* in order to perform the rest of the *tawaaf* and prayer, starting with the *tawaaf* first. It is not necessary for her to repeat the *sa'y*.

358. If the bleeding started after completing the fourth round, but she continued to perform the rites, if she is not *taahir* by the time of *woquf* [in Arafaat] on the 9th day of Dhil-Hejjah, it is recommended that she appoints someone to perform what she has missed in terms of the remainder of the *tawaaf* and its prayer before she leaves [Makkah] for *woquf* in Arafaat. The woman concerned must perform the remainder of the *tawaaf* and its prayer after she is *taahir*.

359. If the bleeding starts after completing the *tawaaf* and before performing its prayer, she is liable to performing the prayer after she is *taahir*, and as a precaution, she should appoint someone to perform the prayer on her behalf.

360. If the bleeding starts before completing the fourth round, i.e. during the first, second, third, or fourth round, she must abort her *tawaaf*, and leave the House immediately. If she became *taahir* before the *woquf* in Arafaat, she must perform the entire *tawaaf* and its prayer, after being *taahir*. If she is not *taahir* by the time of the *woquf*, she has the choice between:

1) Revert her Hajj to Ifraad as mentioned previously, and proceed to Arafaat and [from there to] the Mash'ar al-Haraam and perform all the rites of Mina and the rest of the rites of Makkah. When she completes all the rites of Hajj, she should perform the Mufradah Umrah.

2) Alternatively it is also permissible for her to remain on the Tamattu' [Umrah] and proceed to perform the sa'y and taqseer to be released from the state of ihraam, and then perform the tawaaf and its prayer after becoming taahir.

361. In cases of Istihaadha – undue or lesser menses, if a woman acts according to that that is obligatory for her to do for the obligatory prayers, she would be considered taahir [for the rites of Hajj].

4. Sa'y

362. The fourth rite of the Tamattu' Umrah is the sa'y, which is to walk seven laps between [the mounts of] Safa and Marwah, after performing the tawaaf prayer, and it is considered a rukn or a principal element, such that the Hajj would be void if deliberately abandoned.

363. It is permitted to delay the sa'y to have some rest and cool off, but it is not permitted to delay it to the next day, although it is permitted to delay it until the evening.

364. There is no objection to separate between an obligatory tawaaf and sa'y with a mostahab tawaaf.

365. If one failed to perform the sa'y by forgetting it or due oversight, compulsion, or ignorance of the ruling, he must perform it whenever he remembers. If he had left the city of Makkah, as a precaution he should return to Makkah whenever he remembers the oversight, and perform the sa'y himself if possible. If this proved too hard and difficult for him, he should appoint someone to perform the sa'y on his behalf. One would not be released from his ihraam – even if it was breached – until it [the sa'y] is completely performed by himself or by his agent.

366. It is not conditional in the *sa'y* to attain *tahaarah*, say from *janaabah* or faeces/urine, nor from passing wind, and a woman who is experiencing menses may perform the *sa'y*.

367. It is permitted to perform the *sa'y* while riding an animal or a vehicle or on a wheelchair, or being carried by someone, although walking is the best [option].

368. It is recommended that the vehicle is medium in speed, from Safa to the first landmark[27] – these days marked by green colour fluorescent light – he should brisk walk from the first landmark to the second– also marked by green colour fluorescent light. Brisk walking is not required for women. If he was riding an animal he should make his animal to brisk walk without annoying anyone, and then walk normally from the second landmark to Marwah. He should do the same on return.

The Obligations of *Sa'y*

369. The following are mandatory in *sa'y*

1. *niyyah*
2. starting the *sa'y* from Safa,
3. finishing the *sa'y* at Marwah
4. the number of rounds
5. the normal accepted route
6. facing the destination during each lap
7. legality of the animal used
8. the order of the *sa'y*

1. *Niyyah*

370. [To declare] the *niyyah* for *sa'y* is mandatory, and it must be [declared] at the start of the *sa'y* with the intention of seeking nearness to Allah Almighty. It is preferable to verbally utter the *niyyah* as follows: "I

---

[27] There are two landmarks en route between Safa and Marwah, some 50 yards apart, they are closer to Marwah mount than Safa.

perform the *sa'y* between the Safa and the Marwah seven rounds for the Tamattu' Umrah seeking nearness to Allah Almighty".

2. Starting the *sa'y* from the Safa

371. It is mandatory to start the *sa'y* from the Safa, and for this it is not mandatory to step on the rocks of the mount.

3. Finishing the *sa'y* at the Marwah

372. It is mandatory to finish the *sa'y* at Marwah, and for this it is not mandatory to touch one's toes to the rocks of the mount of Marwah.

373. If he contradicted this and began [the *sa'y*] at Marwah, even by oversight, his *sa'y* is invalidated and as a precaution he should perform a new *sa'y*.

4. The number of rounds

374. It is obligatory to cover the distance between the mounts of Safa and Marwah seven times with nothing more or less. Thus there will be four journeys from Safa to Marwah and three journeys from Marwah to Safa, all together seven rounds.

5. The normally accepted route

375. It is mandatory to go through the route that is normally accepted, thus if he deviated from the route by entering the Mosque and leaving it to re-enter the route of the *sa'y* again, or if he left the route of the *sa'y* to go to the shops and come back to the route of the *sa'y* again, that [excursion] would not be accepted [as part of the *sa'y*]. However, it is permissible to drink water from the designated areas en route.

376. There is no objection to performing the *sa'y* on the first floor or the roof – the second floor – if one opted to do so.

6. Facing the destination

377. In the course of performing the *sa'y,* it is mandatory to be facing the destination, and therefore if he was heading for the mount of Marwah he should be facing Marwah, and if he departed Marwah, heading for Safa, he should be facing Safa. It is not permitted to walk backwards or sideways. There is no objection, however, to turn the head to the left or right, or even to the back, so long as the body is in the direction of the journey of the *sa'y.* While standing, there is no objection to turning the whole body even if that constitute turning one's back to the destination direction, similarly there is no objection if one deviated to the right when coming down from the Safa.

7. Animals or other things used must be legal

378. It is not permitted to perform the *sa'y* on an animal that is usurped and such like. In fact this is applicable to clothing or slippers [worn by the person]. Furthermore, as a precaution, it is also not permitted to even carry anything that is usurped.

8. Order

379. The *sa'y* must be performed after the *tawaaf* and its prayer. It is not permitted to wilfully bring forward the *sa'y* before the *tawaaf,* neither in the Hajj nor in the Umrah. If one deliberately performed the *sa'y* before the *tawaaf* for no reason, he must repeat it. However, if this was for a compelling concern, that should be sufficient. This is also applicable if this was done due to an oversight, although it is recommended to repeat it. The same applies to one who is not conversant with ruling of the case.

380. Continuity is not a requirement for the rounds of *sa'y,* in fact it is permitted for him to engage in prayers, or even eating and drinking for example, or stopping for a rest on either mountain, or in between, and then resuming the *sa'y.*

381. If one started his *sa'y,* and during the *sa'y* he realized that his *tawaaf* was incomplete, if the incompleteness concerned the second half

of the *tawaaf*, he should abort the *sa'y* and go back to complete the *tawaaf*, and then return to complete the *sa'y* from the point he stopped, if he had finished four laps [of the *sa'y*]. The same applies if he had not finished four rounds of the *sa'y*, although it is recommended to renew the *sa'y* altogether. On the other hand, if the incompleteness of his *tawaaf* was more than half, he should also complete the *tawaaf* and then the *sa'y*, even though it is recommended, as a *mostahab* precaution, to renew the *tawaaf* from the beginning and then renew the *sa'y* too. In the case of repeating the *tawaaf* and the *sa'y* without completing them, he may do so with the intention of discharging his duty; whether by completing the remaining ones, or repeating them altogether.

382. If after finishing the *sa'y* he had a doubt about the number of *sa'y* laps [he had done] or its requirements, he should ignore his doubt.

383. If one doubted the number of laps he had done in the course of the *sa'y*, then if he was at Safa and was sure that he had done an even number of rounds but not sure as to whether he had done say four or six rounds, or if he was at Marwah and was sure that he had done an odd number of rounds but not sure as to whether he had done say three or five rounds, he should assume the minimum [number of rounds], and [go on to] complete his *sa'y*, and it is valid.

384. If one doubted the number of rounds he had done in the course of the *sa'y*, but contrary to the case above, in that he was at Safa and was sure that he had done an odd number of rounds, but not sure whether they were three or five, or he was at Marwah and was sure he had done an even number of rounds, but not sure whether they were four or six, his *sa'y* is invalid and he must renew his *sa'y*.

385. If he had a doubt either in Safa or Marwah as to whether he had done an odd or even number of rounds, or if in the middle of *sa'y* route could not tell which direction he should go to – like when stopped for a rest for a while and he wanted to resume his *sa'y* he forgot the direction of his journey – his *sa'y* is invalidated and he must restart the *sa'y* anew.

386. If after completing the *sa'y* he was sure that he had missed one or more laps, it is sufficient for him to perform the lacking ones, and if he could not do so he should assign someone to do it for him by proxy.

5. *Taqseer* or Trimming

387. The fifth rite of the Tamattu' Umrah, which is its final obligation, is the *taqseer* or Trimming. The Trimming must be performed after completing the *sa'y*, and by doing so one is released from the state and therefore restrictions of the *ihraam*, [this release is known in Arabic as *Ihlaal*].

388. The *taqseer* is accomplished by trimming some hair from the head or the beard (if applicable), or some of the finger or toenails. This may be performed anywhere and it is not necessary to be performed immediately. [Until the Haajj performs this rite, he would not be released from *ihraam*, and therefore the sooner he performs this rite the better.]

389. It is not permitted to shave the head in the Tamattu' Umrah, and if he does he must give a *kaffaarah* of a sheep. This is applicable, as a precaution, even if he did so due to an oversight or ignorance of the ruling. If one shaved part of his head he is not liable to the *kaffaarah*.

390. At the time of performing the *taqseer* one must state the *niyyah* which is, "I perform the *taqseer* for *ihlaal* from the *ihraam* of the Tamattu' Umrah seeking nearness to Allah Almighty".

391. When one has performed the *taqseer*, everything that was prohibited for him as a result of the *ihraam* becomes permissible, even sexual intercourse with one's spouse. It is not mandatory, nor is it a legal requirement, to perform *Tawaaf al-Nisa'* in the Tamattu' Umrah, and

thus [after *taqseer*] a wife becomes *halaal* for her husband and a husband becomes *halaal* for his wife, without the need for *Tawaaf al-Nisa*[28].

392. One who fails to perform the *taqseer* until he declares and assumes *ihraam* for the Hajj, and headed for Arafaat, if this [failure] was due to an oversight or ignorance, his Tamattu' Umrah is correct, but he must give a *kaffaarah* of a sheep, as a precaution. If his failure was deliberate, his Tamattu' Umrah is invalidated and his Hajj is reverted to Ifraad, he thus must perform the rest of the rites in the order [required], and he should perform his Hajj in the following year.

393. If one deliberately engages in sexual intercourse before performing the *taqseer*, s/he is liable to *kaffaarah*.

394. If a pilgrim releases himself [from the *ihraam*] after performing the *tawaaf* prayer of his Tamattu' Umrah and before performing the *taqseer*, he is still not discharged from his *ihraam*, and his case is that of a *muhrim* who has committed some of the prohibited acts while in the state of *ihraam*.

Miscellaneous issues

395. After completing the rites of Tamattu' Umrah, the pilgrim must wait until the time for declaring and assuming the *ihraam* for the Hajj. It is recommended that he declares and assumes *ihraam* on the eighth day of Dhil-Hejjah, otherwise it would be obligatory to do so on the ninth in preparation for performing the rites of the Hajj.

396. It is permitted to leave the holy city of Makkah – after completing the Tamattu' Umrah and before the Hajj – for a long or short distance without *ihraam*, although it is *makruh* – discouraged – to do so. However, it is permitted for one to leave [Makkah] for the suburbs of Makkah and Mina, without it being *makruh*.

---

[28] *Tawaaf al-Nisa'* is only applicable for the Tamattu' Hajj, and husband and wife only become *halaal* to each other after performing this *tawaaf* and its prayer.

The Rites of the Tamattu' Hajj

397. The rites of Hajj of TAMATTU' are thirteen:

1. *Ihraam.*
2. *Woquf* or staying in Arafaat.
3. *Woquf* or staying in Mash'ar.
4. *Ram'y* or stoning of Jamarat al-Aqabah in Mina.
5. *Had'y* or slaughter of the sacrifice in Mina.
6. *Halq / taqseer* or the shaving of the head or trimming its hair in Mina.
7. *Tawaaf al-Ziyaarah.*
8. *Salaat al-tawaaf* or the *tawaaf* prayer.
9. *Sa'y.*
10. *Tawaaf al-Nisa'.*
11. *Salaat Tawaaf al-Nisa'* or the *tawaaf* prayer.
12. *Mabeet* or staying over night in Mina.
13. *Ram'y* or stoning of the three Jamaraat.

1. *Ihraam* of the Tamattu' Hajj

398. The first of the Hajj rites is the *ihraam*, which is obligatory for the Tamattu' Hajj, and in fact it is a *rukn* – a principal element, and the Hajj is invalidated if deliberately abandoned.

399. The process of the *ihraam* is the same as that for the Umrah, as mentioned previously, with the exception of the *niyyah* and the place of [declaring and assuming] *ihraam*. The *niyyah* or intention is to state, "*I declare and assume the ihraam for the TAMATTU' HAJJ seeking nearness to Allah Almighty*". As for the place of *ihraam*, one must do so in the holy city of Makkah.

400. The first time one can declare and assume the *ihraam* is after completing the rites of Umrah, and the time of [declaring] *ihraam* extends to the ninth day of Dhil-Hejjah, which is the day of *woquf* in Arafaat, when it becomes obligatory upon the pilgrim to declare and assume *ihraam* so that he can observe the *woquf* in time.

401. [The pilgrim] declares and assumes the state of *ihraam* for the Tamattu' Hajj from the holy city of Makkah, and it is preferable to do so from Masgid al-Haraam, preferably from Hijr Isma'el or Maqaam Ibrahim peace be upon them. He should wear the two garments of *ihraam*, and then declares the *niyyah* of *ihraam* for the Hajj as mentioned previously, and then utters the *talbiyah* as previously mentioned. [Case # 166].

402. If one forgot to declare and assume the *ihraam* from the holy city of Makkah, and he left Makkah on the eighth day for Mina or Arafaat, and then remembered the oversight, it is obligatory for him to return to Makkah to declare and assume the *ihraam* there. The same applies if he left Makkah without declaring and assuming *ihraam* due to not being conversant with the ruling of the case. He should return to Makkah to declare *ihraam* there, if possible.

403. He who is obliged to return to Makkah to declare and assume *ihraam*, if he is excused from doing so, or in doing so he would not be able to come back to Arafaat in time for the Designated (*ikhtiari*)[29] *woquf* on the ninth day, which is from noon to sunset, he must declare and assume the *ihraam* from the spot remembered or realised this, and this would be sufficient for him.

404. If one did not remember his failure to declare and assume *ihraam* until after completing all of the rites, his Hajj is correct if this was due to oversight or ignorance.

405. If one deliberately failed to declare and assume *ihraam* until he missed the time for the two *woquf's,* his Hajj is invalidated, and so too if one had not assumed *ihraam*, due to oversight or ignorance, and after

---

[29] The Haajj (pilgrim) is obliged to perform certain rites during particular Designated times specified for different rites and sites. If under certain circumstances s/he fails to perform those rites during their relevant Designated times, then s/he must perform those missed rites during their relevant Emergency times.

being reminded he did not declare and assume *ihraam* when it was possible for him to do so.

2. *Woquf* in Arafaat

406. The second rite of the Hajj is *Woquf* in Arafaat. It is obligatory for the *Haajj* (pilgrim) to observe *Woquf* [being preset] in Arafaat, in that he is present there all the time from midday or noontime until sunset, [referred to as the Designated (*ikhtiari*) *woquf*]. This does not mean that he should stand on his feet.

407. It is obligatory to observe the *Woquf* in Arafaat itself, for it is not sufficient to observe the *Woquf* in Namirah, or other areas in the vicinity of Arafaat. Arafaat has known borders with clear visible signs stating "The Start of Arafaat" and "The End of Arafaat", and therefore one may not breach those borders.

408. The *rukn,* or principal element of the *woquf* is the extent that can be called as *woquf,* which literally means "being present there"[30], and the time that exceeds the *rukn* is obligatory, and it is not permitted to abandon the excess time. BUT if one [deliberately] abandons the *rukn* – the basic *woquf* itself until time of the Designated *woquf* has lapsed, until sunset, his Hajj is invalidated, and neither the Emergency *woquf* [in Arafaat] nor that in Mash'ar would be of any use to him.

409. The Emergency *Woquf* in Arafaat is from the time of sunset [on the ninth day] until the time of Fajr on the day of Eid [the tenth day].

410. If one forgets to observe the *woquf* in Arafaat [on time], it is obligatory for him to do so in the Designated time if it was possible, failing that, he should observe the Emergency *woquf*, and then observe the *woquf* in the Mash'ar and his Hajj is valid.

---

[30] Being present in Arafaat even for a few minutes constitutes the *rukn* of *woquf,* and if one after, say, ten minutes left Arafaat, he has disobeyed the orders of Allah Almighty and has sinned, but his Hajj would not be invalidated.

411. As mentioned previously, it is obligatory [for the pilgrim] to observe the *woquf* in Arafaat [during the entire period] from midday noontime / midday until sunset. If, due to deliberate failure, one did not observe the *woquf* on time, [i.e. not from precisely noontime, but from later on], he has sinned but his Hajj is correct and he is not liable [to do or give] anything. However, if this was due to an oversight or another excuse, he has not sinned, and his Hajj is correct too.

412. If one did not observe the *woquf* in Arafaat up to the end of the required time, i.e. he deliberately left Arafaat before sunset, if he repented and returned before sunset, he is not liable to a *kaffaarah*, and if he does not repent and does not return, he is liable to a *kaffaarah* of a camel. If he could not afford a camel, he must fast 18 days continually with no interruption between those days. The fast can be in Makkah, en route back to his hometown or when at home.

413. If due to oversight one departed [Arafaat] before sunset and did not realise this during the time [before sunset] he is not liable to anything. If he realised the oversight before sunset, it is obligatory for him to return to Arafaat, and to remain there until sunset. If he dos not do so and does not return, he has sinned and the ruling of his case is similar to the one who deliberately left Arafaat. The ruling of the one who does so out of ignorance is the same as that who had forgotten, even if his ignorance being due to him being *moqassir*.

414. The Designated *woquf* for Arafaat – as mentioned before – is from midday to sunset, and the Emergency *Woquf* is from sunset to *fajr*. The latter is qualifying for anyone who forgot to observe the *woquf* in Arafaat, or was excused due to any other reason. However, in the case of the Emergency *Woquf* it is not obligatory to observe it completely and entirely[31] as it is required in the case of the Designated *woquf*. The obligation in this [Emergency *Woquf*] is the extent that can be called as "being present there". However, the Emergency *Woquf* is a substitute for the Designated *woquf* as far as the obligation of observing the entire

---

[31] i.e. from sunset to *fajr*.

93

period is concerned, if it was possible to do so. This is provided this would not detract him from [the *woquf*] in the Mash'ar before sunrise.

415. If one observed the Emergency *Woquf* [in Arafaat], and it was not possible for him to observe the *woquf* in the Mash'ar before sunrise, his Hajj is invalidated by deliberately failing to observe the *woquf* in the Mash'ar. Therefore it is obligatory for him, if it was possible, to ensure that he observes the *woquf* in the Mash'ar, by observing the Emergency *woquf* in Arafaat, and then come to the Mash'ar. If that was not possible, he should limit [his *woquf*] to observing the *woquf* in the Mash'ar [only], and [go on] to complete his Hajj. Similarly, if he missed observing the *woquf* in Arafaat completely due to forgetting, oversight or any other reason, and he did not remember it until after the elapse of the *woquf* time, but it was possible for him to observe the *Woquf* in the Mash'ar in the Designated time, his *woquf* in the Mash'ar is qualifying and his Hajj is valid.

416. The above ruling concerning the one who had forgotten applies to the *qaasir* ignorant, but as for the *moqassir*, the ruling in this case is inconclusive [i.e. no *fatwa* is given in the validity or invalidity of the Hajj].

417. If the judge or mufti of the non-Shi'a announced the day of Arafaat and the day of Eid, and one is not sure of the invalidity of the announcement, or if one was sure of the invalidity of the announcement but was confined to comply with that, then it is permissible for him to follow accordingly for the two *woquf*'s, and the Hajj is valid and he does not need to repeat.

3. *Woquf* in the Mash'ar al-Haraam

418. The third rite of the Hajj is the *Woquf* in the Mash'ar al-Haraam. Mash'ar al-Haraam is also known as al-Muzdalafah and Juma', and it is located between Arafaat and Mina, and there are signs indicating its borders.

419. It is obligatory to observe the *woquf* in Mash'ar al-Haraam after departing from Arafaat on the eve of the Eid, and as a precaution one should observe *mabeet*[32] and at the break of Fajr one should declare the intention by stating, "*Aqifu* (I remain) in the Mash'ar al-Haraam from the *Fajr* to Sunrise, for the Tamattu' Hajj seeking nearness to Allah." If he departs from it [Mash'ar al-Haraam] and went beyond the Mohassar valley before sunrise, he has sinned, and he should give a *kaffaarah* of a sheep as a precaution.

420. The entire *woquf* in the Mash'ar is obligatory and what can be called as *woquf* or "being there" is a *rukn* (principal element of the *woquf*). Thus he who completely abandons to observe it would invalidate his Hajj, and if he became insane or lost consciousness, or fell asleep, etc. after he observed what could be called as *woquf*, that would be sufficient to him in discharging his due in this respect. But if the above-mentioned scenarios happened to him during the entire period, as a precaution, his *woquf* is invalidated in certain cases, [but not always, the details of which are beyond the scope of this presentation].

421. The *Woquf* in the Mash'ar is not meant to be standing on the feet, but it is sufficient for one to be there, regardless of whether he was sitting or standing, sleeping or awake, or walking or moving from one place to another.

422. It is permissible to depart Mash'ar for Mina before the break of dawn for women, children, the elderly, and the sick for whom the congestion [of the day] would cause too much hardship for them. Also it is permitted to depart for those who have an urgent business to do.

423. If one does not manage to observe the *woquf* in the Mash'ar during the designated time, it is sufficient for him to observe the *woquf* there, even for a short time, before noontime / midday [on the day of Eid].

---

[32] The reference to *mabeet* in Mash'ar al-Haraam points to the requirement of being there for the entire period, whereas the *woquf* points to being there for only a short period of time, like the case of the women and children and the elderly, who can stay there for a relatively brief period to be considered as *woquf* and then depart for Mina.

424. There are three specific times for the *woquf* in Mash'ar:

    I.   The Eve of the *Eid*, for one who is unable to observe *woquf* after the break of *Fajr*, as mentioned before.

    II. Between the break of *Fajr* and sunrise.

    III. Between sunrise and midday / noontime.

425. For each of the *woquf's* in Arafaat and Mash'ar there are two categories: the Designated (*ikhtiari*) and the Emergency. Depending on the success or failure of the pilgrim in observing the two *woquf's*, and their respective categories, the following could arise:

    I.   The pilgrim observes both *woquf's* in their Designated times, and there is no problem with his Hajj.

    II. The pilgrim does not observe either of them at all, his Hajj is invalid, and thus he should perform the Mufradah Umrah with the *ihraam* he assumed for the Hajj.

    III. The pilgrim observes the Designated *Woquf* in Arafaat and Emergency *Woquf* in the Mash'ar, and his Hajj is valid.

    IV. The opposite of case # III (above), i.e. the pilgrim observes the Emergency *Woquf* in Arafaat and Designated *Woquf* in the Mash'ar, and his Hajj is valid.

    V. The pilgrim observes the Emergency *Woquf* in both [i.e. Arafaat and the Mash'ar], and his Hajj is valid.

    VI. The pilgrim observes the Designated *Woquf* in Arafaat only, and his Hajj is valid.

    VII. The pilgrim observes the Designated *Woquf* in Mash'ar only, and his Hajj is valid.

    VIII. The pilgrim observes the Emergency *Woquf* in Arafaat only, and his Hajj is invalid.

    IX. The pilgrim observes the Emergency *Woquf* in Mash'ar only, thus his Hajj is valid.

426. It is recommended that [while] in the Mash'ar al-Haraam, one should collect the stones [required] for the *Ram'y* [or the stoning of the Jamaraat], and it is permissible to take more than that is required, and it is

permissible for others to collect for him, and if he ran out of stones, he may collect stones from the valley of Mohassar or from Mina.

427. After the sunrise on the day of Eid, it is obligatory for the pilgrim to depart from Mash'ar al-Haraam for Mina to perform its rites, which are the *Ram'y* [stoning], *Had'y* [sacrifice], and *Halq* [shaving], which are the fourth, fifth, and sixth rites of the Hajj.

4 – 6. Rites of Mina

4. Ram'y [stoning] of Jamarat-al-'Aqabah

428. The fourth rite of Hajj is the *Ram'y*. When the pilgrim arrives in Mina he should first go to Jamarat-al-'Aqabah, which is the first obelisk, also known as al- Jamarat-al-Kubra – The Greater Obelisk. The pilgrim should stone this obelisk with seven stones that he collected from the Mash'ar, or from within the borders of the sacred Haram.

429. The time for the *Ram'y* [stoning] of the first obelisk is on the Day of Eid, from sunrise to sunset. The *Ram'y* is the first of the rites of Mina, and thus it is not permissible, as a precaution, to bring forward any of the other rites, namely the *Had'y* and the *halq*.

Obligations of the Ram'y

430. A number of issues are obligatory in *Ram'y*:

    I.   *niyyah* or intention,
   II.   number [of stoning],
  III.   hitting of the Jamara,
  IV.   sequence of stoning,
   V.   *Ram'y* during the day.

1. *Niyyah*

431. [Declaring] the *niyyah* or intention is mandatory in *Ram'y*, and it should be declared at the time of the first throw, and continue to be the

same to the last one. It is preferable for the Haajj (pilgrim) to utter *niyyah* by saying, "*Armi* (I stone) Jamarat-al-'Aqabah seven times seeking nearness to Allah Almighty".

2. The Number of Stoning

432. It is obligatory that the *Ram'y* consists of throwing seven stones, and therefore if they were less than that, it would not be qualifying, and he must ensure to make up for the missing ones. On the other hand, if one threw more than seven, [doing so] as a precaution, then there is no objection to that.

3. Hitting the Jamara

433. It is obligatory in the *Ram'y*, that the Jamara, or its location, is hit with every one of the seven stones in that *Ram'y*. If one [of the stones] went astray, it is mandatory to attempt another throw so that it hits the Jamara. [The stones] reaching [the Jamara, as opposed to hitting it] is not sufficient, nor is placing the stones on the target, [as opposed to throwing them].

434. If one threw the stone at the Jamara, and it hit something en route, but it still hit the Jamara, then there is no objection to that, and it counts [as one hit]. Unless the stone bounced off something that is solid such as another stone, and eventually hit the Jamara, in this case this does not qualify [as a hit], as a precaution.

435. If during the process of the *Ram'y*, the Raami [the person performing the *Ram'y* - throwing the stones] doubted whether the stone(s) hit the Jamara, he should assume not and throw others instead.

436. If after completing the *Ram'y* he doubted whether he had hit the Jamara or not, he should ignore his doubt, regardless of his doubt being about the number of hits or any other obligatory aspect of the *Ram'y*.

437. It is permissible in general to perform the *Ram'y* from the upper level, instead of the ground level, whether out of choice or due to

compulsion. Also it is permissible to hit the extensions of the column of the Jamara, longitudinally or latitudinally.

4. Sequential order

438. It is mandatory that the *Ram'y* is done in sequential order, i.e. to throw the seven stones one-by-one each hitting [the Jamara]. It would not be acceptable if one threw the seven stones all at once, even if all seven hit [the target]. Similarly it would not be acceptable if one threw two or more stones at a time.

439. It is not mandatory to throw the stone with the right hand, and one is permitted to do so with the left hand, even by choice. Although throwing by the right hand is preferred.

5. To perform the Ram'y during the day

440. It is obligatory to perform the *Ram'y* during the daylight, i.e. from sunrise to sunset. However, if one cannot observe the Designated *woquf* in Mash'ar al-Haraam, and observed the Emergency *woquf* during the night, and entered Mina, it is permissible for him to perform the *Ram'y* during the night, like the women, children, the elderly, and the sick.

441. If due to an excuse one performed the *Ram'y* during the night, but during the day his excuse was no more, he is not obliged to repeat the *Ram'y*, although as a precaution it is [recommended to do so].

Some of the Conditions of the Ram'y

442. [When collecting the stones, one should consider] some of the conditions of the stones collected for the *Ram'y*:

- the stones should be virgin, i.e. they should not have been used for *Ram'y* previously,
- they should be of an average size, neither too big nor too small, but the size of a finger segment,
- they should be stones or pebbles but not clay or dried mud,

- it is not necessary for them to be *taahir*,
- they must be collected from the Haram district.

443. Continuity between the seven throws is not conditional, and one may have a slight rest in the process. However, if the time gap was long, he must, as a precaution, renew the Ram'y again. Similarly continuity is not conditional for the three Jamaraat, i.e. one can perform the *Ram'y* on the first in the morning, the second by midday, and the third before sunset. This latter case is applicable to the 11th and the 12th day, when one must perform the *Ram'y* on all three Jamaraat.

5. *Had'y* or Sacrifice

444. The fifth rite of the Hajj is the *Had'y*, which is the slaughter of the animal that takes place after performing the *Ram'y*.

445. For the *Had'y* it is obligatory to offer one animal, and it is recommended to offer more, without limit. The *Had'y* is obligatory in the Tamattu' Hajj, even if the Hajj was a *mostahab* one, and even, as a precaution, if one was from the people of Makkah. As for the *qaarin*, the one performing the Qiraan Hajj, the *Had'y* is also obligatory as he brings the *Had'y* with him. The exception is the Ifraad Hajj where a *had'y* is not required.

446. If an animal is not available for slaughter or the Haajj (pilgrim) cannot find an animal, even though he has the money to cover the cost, and he decided to go back home, he must leave the money with someone he trusts to buy and slaughter the animal on his behalf, during the month of Dhil-Hejjah. If he could not do so in that year, he must do so in the following year in the month of Dhil-Hejjah.

447. One *Had'y* must be offered by one person only, thus it is not permitted for two or more individuals to share one *Had'y*, under normal circumstances. If there is a necessity [to share one *had'y*], as a precaution, [the individuals] should offer both the *Had'y* [the shared one]

as well as each fasting [ten days][33]. This is applicable to the obligatory Hajj, however, in the case of *mostahab* Hajj; it is permissible to share one *Had'y*.

448. If one bought a *Had'y* and then lost it, he must buy a second one, but if he found the lost one, he must slaughter the one he had lost, and, as a precaution, it is recommended that he should also slaughter the second one too. If he slaughtered the second one before finding the one he had lost, it is preferred, but in fact obligatory as a precaution, to it too.

Obligations of the Had'y

449. The obligations of the *Had'y* are:

    I.   The *niyyah*
    II. That it is a cattle
    III. That it is of a certain age
    IV. That it is of sound creation – without any defects of missing limbs
    V. That the slaughter is carried out on the day of Eid
    VI. That the slaughter takes place in Mina
    VII. To observe the order, as a precaution
    VIII. That it is not taken outside the [limits] of the Haram

1. The *niyyah*

450. The *niyyah* is obligatory for the slaughter, and it is preferred to utter it by saying, "*Adhbahu* (I slaughter) the *Had'y* seeking nearness to Allah Almighty".

451. If one does not carry out the slaughter himself, both he and the person carrying out the slaughter should utter the *niyyah*. If only he uttered the intention, and not the slaughterer, this is sufficient.

---

[33] Three days of which should be performed during the Hajj season, and the remaining seven when they go back home.

2. That it is a cattle

452. It is obligatory that the *Had'y* is a cattle, i.e. it is a camel, cow, sheep, and the goat is considered from [the category of] the sheep.

3. That it is of a certain age

453. The age of the *Had'y* is sufficient if it is called, [in each case] a camel, or a cow, or a sheep, or a goat, and it is not sufficient if it is of a young age such that, in each case, it is referred to as young weaning camel, or calf, or lamb, or kid. As a recommended precaution,

- the camel must have completed five years and entered the age of six,
- the cow has completed two years of age,
- the sheep has completed seven months, although [it is better] to have completed one year of age and has entered the second,
- the goat has completed two years of age.

4. To be of complete creation

454. It is obligatory that the *Had'y* is of complete creation, and therefore it does not qualify if the animal is one-eyed, or lame, or too old, or of broken inner part of the horn[34], or of missing ears or any other limb, or castrated, or thin/skinny.

455. As a precaution, it is recommended that the *Had'y* is not hornless or earless by birth. However, it is permissible if the ear was pierced or slit, without anything missing from it. Similarly, [it is permissible] if the [animal's] exterior [part of the] horn is broken, or if the sheep does not have a fat-tail by birth.

---

[34] i.e. the horn is uprooted.

456. The conditions specified for the *Had'y* are applicable if these are possible, otherwise if it is not possible [to obtain a perfect match] but the imperfect, then that should be sufficient.

5. The slaughter should be on the day of Eid

457. It is obligatory that the slaughter [of the animal] takes place on the day of Eid, or during the daytime on the Days of Tashreeq, which are the 10th, 11th, and 12th of Dhil-Hejjah, and it is permissible to delay the slaughter beyond these days. However, if one delayed this due to an excuse or deliberately, he has until the end of Dhil-Hejjah to do so and that would be sufficient, although this delay constitutes a sin [for the one who deliberately delayed this rite].

6. The slaughter should take place in Mina

458. It is obligatory for the slaughter to take place in Mina, and it is not permissible to do so elsewhere. It is permissible to carry out the slaughter in the new slaughterhouses, which are said to be outside the limits of Mina, if there were any confinement, restriction, or difficulty, etc.

7. Observing the order as a precaution

459. In carrying out the slaughter of the *Had'y* it is obligatory to observe the order prescribed for it, as a precaution; that the slaughter should be done after the *Ram'y* and before the *halq* (the shaving or trimming of the hair). If one breached this order due to an oversight, ignorance, or forgetting it, or due to confinement or difficulty, then there is no objection to it.

8. Not to take it outside the Haram

460. It is obligatory that one does not take any meat of the sacrifice outside the Haram. However, if there is no use or consumption for it, it is permitted to take it outside. It is also permitted [to take it outside] if the

Haajj (pilgrim) bought the [sacrificed] *Had'y* – that he had previously given it to a destitute.

Miscellaneous issues

461. If one slaughtered an animal assuming that it is well-nourished, but then it turned out to be skinny, this is satisfactory and he is not obliged to slaughter another one.

462. It is a recommended precaution for the Haajj (pilgrim) to eat from the slaughtered animal, and offers some of it to a Mu'min (a believer) – even if he is well off – or to his agent, and offer some other part of the slaughtered animal to a destitute believer or his agent. The amount of the gift and the charity should be one third of the slaughtered animal, and it is permissible to give [some] as charity to another Haajj (pilgrim) who is not well off.

463. If one could not find the perfect *Had'y*, but managed to find the imperfect one, he should give preference to it over fasting. If he could not find the *Had'y* and its cost, he must revert to fasting, if he is able to [fast]. If he could not find the *Had'y* only, but could afford its cost, he must deposit the cost with someone to buy the *Had'y* during Dhil-Hejjah, if he were not to stay until the end of Dhil-Hejjah. If the agent found a *Had'y* during the month of Dhil-Hejjah he should slaughter it, otherwise he should delay it until the following year. If by then he could not find it he should fast.

464. If one could not find the *Had'y* and could not afford its cost, he should fast ten days; three during Hajj [season], and seven days when he returns home. It is obligatory to fast the three days during Dhil-Hejjah. If he could not afford the *Had'y*, or its cost, or its alternative, i.e. the fast, he is not obliged to anything and nor is his heir / eldest son.

465. If one fasted three days and then found a *Had'y* during Dhil-Hejjah, then he is not obliged to offer the *Had'y*, although it is preferential to do so.

466. If one dies before sending a *Had'y* to Mina [for slaughter], and he was obliged to do so, his heirs must take the cost of the *Had'y* from what he has left behind to buy a *Had'y* for this purpose.

6. *Halq* or *Taqseer* (Shaving or Trimming)

467. The sixth rite of the Hajj is shaving or trimming on the day of Eid in Mina, and that must be done after the *Ram'y* and the *Had'y*. It is permitted to bring it forward before *Had'y* if there are grounds for confinement and hardship.

468. The *halq* consists of shaving the head entirely, and the *taqseer* is to trim some of the hair of the head or beard, or moustache, or trim some of the fingernails.

469. Using hair-cutting machine at fine scale qualifies for shaving.

470. A male [pilgrim] has the option between shaving or trimming, if the Hajj was his first, although shaving is preferred in general, especially on the first Hajj.

471. If one was an agent on behalf of someone else, the agent is obliged to the rulings that apply to himself, so for example, if the agent was on his second or more Hajj, he has the choice between shaving or trimming even if he was acting on behalf of someone for his first Hajj.

472. All of the above applies to male pilgrims, as for female pilgrims, they are obliged to trimming, and they are not obliged to shaving at all, and in fact it is forbidden for them to do so. They should trim some of their hair or clip their fingernails as mentioned previously for the Umrah.

Nevertheless, it is permitted for women to perform the *Ram'y* on the Eve of the Eid, and then [followed by] the *taqseer* in Mina during the night, and then to go to Makkah to perform the two *tawaaf's* and the *sa'y*, on the Eve of the Eid, and it is not mandatory for them to wait until the daylight. Needless to say they are obliged to appoint an agent to slaughter the *Had'y* on the day of the Eid.

473. *halq* is waved for he who does not have hair on his head, and he is obliged to perform the *taqseer* or trimming, but as a recommended precaution, he should regardless apply the shaving razor or the fine hair cutting machine to his head too.

Obligations of the *halq* and *taqseer*

474. The obligations of the *halq* and *taqseer* are three:

    I.   to be in Mina
    II. the *niyyah*
    III. the order, as a precaution

1. Being in Mina

475. It is obligatory that the *halq* or *taqseer* is performed in Mina, and it is not permissible elsewhere.

476. If one left Mina without performing the *halq* or *taqseer*, whether deliberately, or due to an oversight or forgetting, it is mandatory for him to return to Mina to perform the *halq* or *taqseer*, if this was possible, otherwise he should do so where he is, and it is desirable to send his hair or fingernails to Mina to be buried or dropped there.

2. The *niyyah*

477. It is obligatory to have the *niyyah* or the intention for the *halq* or the *taqseer*, just like any other acts of worship or rite. For *halq*, he should say, "I perform the *halq* as part of the Hajj duty, seeking nearness to Allah Almighty." In the case of trimming – *taqseer* – one should use the word *taqseer* instead of *halq* in the *niyyah* declaration.

3. Order

478. As a precaution, one should observe the order for the *halq* / *taqseer*, in that they should be performed after the [slaughter of the] *Had'y*. If one contravened that either deliberately or due to an oversight or ignorance,

106

he is not obliged to anything. Although in the case of deliberate contravention, or that without an excuse, one should as an obligatory precaution, repeat it such that the order is maintained.

479. It is obligatory to observe the order of the *halq / taqseer* in that it should be executed before performing the *Tawaaf al-Ziyaarah*, which will be mentioned *InSha'Allah*. Thus if one performed the *tawaaf* before *halq / taqseer,* he should repeat [them in the correct order] even if his action was due to oversight.

Miscellaneous issues

480. If one completed the three rites of Mina; the *Ram'y* of Jamarat-al-Aqabah, the *Had'y* slaughter, and the *halq / taqseer,* all restrictions due to *ihraam* are lifted with the exception of [wearing] perfume and [contact with] women. Hunting is also forbidden for him, although this is not due to *ihraam*, but because of Makkah, as hunting in Makkah is prohibited. However, it is *makruh* – discouraged – for a man to cover his head or wear sewn clothing before performing *Tawaaf al-Ziyaarah* and its prayer.

481. If [the pilgrim] returned to Makkah and performed *Tawaaf al-Ziyaarah* and its two-*rak'ah* prayer, and then performed the *sa'y* between Safa and Marwah, then wearing perfume becomes permissible for him, although it is *makruh* – discouraged. Then if he performed *Tawaaf al-Nisa'* and its two-*rak'ah* prayer, women become permissible for him too [i.e. sexual contact with one's spouse becomes permissible]. At that stage he is released from any restriction that was imposed on him due to *ihraam*. Hunting remains forbidden for him, not due to *ihraam* but because it is one of the prohibited acts of the Haram as mentioned earlier.

7. Tawaaf al-Ziyaarah

482. The seventh act of the Hajj is *Tawaaf al-Ziyaarah* also known as *Tawaaf al-Hajj*. After performing the rites of Mina, it is obligatory to return to the holy city of Makkah to perform the rest of the obligatory rites.

483. *Tawaaf al-Ziyaarah* is like the *tawaaf* in the Tamattu' Umrah, and its obligations are like those of the latter too, as well as the acts that are *mostahab* or *makruh*, or those acts that invalidate it. The only exception is the *niyyah*, which should be uttered as follows: "I perform *tawaaf* around this House seven rounds [for] *Tawaaf al-Ziyaarah* for the Tamattu' Hajj seeking nearness to Allah Almighty".

8. The Prayer of *Tawaaf al-Ziyaarah*

484. The eighth rite of the Hajj is the *Salaat* or prayer of *Tawaaf al-Ziyaarah*. After completing *Tawaaf al-Ziyaarah*, it is obligatory to perform two-*rak'ah* prayer of the *tawaaf* by Maqaam Ibrahim *alayhis-salam* or behind it, as mentioned for the prayer of the Umrah *tawaaf*. The only exception is the *niyyah*, in which he should state; "I perform two *rak'ah* of prayer of *Tawaaf al-Ziyaarah*, seeking nearness to Allah Almighty".

9. *Sa'y* between Safa and Marwah

485. The ninth rite of the Hajj is the *sa'y* between Safa and Marwah, which is exactly like the *sa'y* for the Tamattu' Umrah, with the exception of the *niyyah*, which should read, "I perform the *sa'y* between the Safa and Marwah for the Tamattu' Hajj seeking nearness to Allah Almighty".

486. Contrary to that of the Umrah, this *sa'y* is not followed by *taqseer*.

10 – 11. *Tawaaf al-Nisa'* and its prayer

487. The tenth and eleventh rites of the Hajj are *Tawaaf al-Nisa'* and its prayer, which come after the *sa'y*. Neither women are *halaal* for men, nor men are for women until after this *tawaaf* and its prayer [are performed].

488. *Tawaaf al-Nisa'* and its prayer is just like *Tawaaf al-Ziyaarah* and its prayer, with the exception of the *niyyah*. He declares the *niyyah* for *Tawaaf al-Nisa'* by stating, "I perform *Tawaaf al-Nisa'* seven rounds seeking nearness to Allah Almighty", and for its prayer, the *niyyah* is "I

perform the two *rak'ah* prayer of *Tawaaf al-Nisa'* seeking nearness to Allah Almighty".

489. The obligation of *Tawaaf al-Nisa'* and its prayer is applicable to all regardless of their age or their state of mind, etc. It is obligatory upon everyone whether the [pilgrim] is young or old, adolescent or under age, even if the child is so young that he does not distinguish the good and bad, etc. or whether the pilgrim is sane or insane, whose guardian declared the *ihraam* for him, and the free or slave, who declared *ihraam* with the permission of his master.

490. The distinguishing child [should] perform the *tawaaf* himself as well as its prayer, but in the case of the non-distinguishing child, his guardian should perform the *tawaaf* and its prayer on his behalf. If the distinguishing child, or the guardian of the non-distinguishing child failed to perform *Tawaaf al-Nisa'*, [in each case] the child shall remain in his state of *ihraam*, thus women[35] are not halaal to him until he performs the *tawaaf* himself, or seek an agent to do so after [the child reaches] the age of adolescence, and it is permissible for the guardian to seek an agent before [the child reaches] the age of adolescence.

491. If one ignored *Tawaaf al-Nisa'* either by forgetting about it or due to an oversight, but instead performed *Tawaaf al-Widaa'* – the Farewell *tawaaf*, due to a misunderstanding in doing so, this should qualify, even though, as a precaution, [he should] repeat it or get someone to do it [repeat *Tawaaf al-Nisa'*] on his behalf.

492. If he does not come to Makkah on the tenth day after completing the rites of Mina [for that day], he should come to Makkah the following day or the day after to perform what he is liable to in terms of the rites of Makkah. As a *mostahab* precaution, he should come back to Makkah for the *tawaaf* and its prayer before midday on the 13th, even though it is permissible to delay this until the end of the month of Dhil-Hejjah.

493. After completing the rites of Makkah, which are

---

[35] or vice versa.

109

- *Tawaaf al-Ziyaarah* and its prayer,
- *Sa'y* between the Safa and Marwah,
- *Tawaaf al-Nisa'* and its prayer,

If he performed them on the day of Eid, or the following day, he must go back to Mina to complete the rest of the rites of Mina, and to observe the *mabeet* there as mentioned in the following section *InSha'Allah*.

Miscellaneous issues

494. It is not permissible to voluntary perform *Tawaaf al-Ziyaarah* and its *sa'y* prior to the two *Woquf*'s in Arafaat and Mash'ar, and the rites of Mina. It is permissible under exceptional circumstances, but if one voluntarily performed the *tawaaf* and the *sa'y*, they would be null and void.

495. If one is compelled to bring forward the *tawaaf* and the *sa'y*, then it is permissible to do so. For example if a woman knew that her menses would start after the rites of Mina, and it would not be possible for her to remain until she is cleansed, as her tour party would not wait for her, then it is permissible for her to perform the *tawaaf* prior to the two *woquf's*. The same is applicable to a woman [who is experiencing] postpartum, as well as the sick and the elderly, etc. who may not be able to perform the *tawaaf* after completing the rites in Mina due to overcrowding. It is therefore permissible for them all to perform the *tawaaf* prior to the two *woquf's* and the rites of Mina.

496. If the above excused were able to perform the *tawaaf* after their return from Mina, they should repeat the *tawaaf* and the *sa'y* as it is a precaution and a priority for them.

12. *Mabeet* in Mina

497. The twelfth rite of the Hajj is the *mabeet* [stay] in Mina, for it is obligatory on the eve of the 11th and 12th, and on certain occasions on the eve of the 13th too.

498. It is obligatory to observe the *mabeet* on the eve of the 13th if the sun of the 12th day set while he had not left Mina, or if he did not abstain from women[36] or hunting. However, if one had abstained from women and hunting, or the sun did not set while he was in Mina, it is permitted for him to leave Mina, after midday / noontime on the 12th [of Dhil-Hejjah]. If one deliberately leaves Mina before midday of the 12th, he has sinned and must return before noontime if possible. In the case of forgetting or oversight, there is no liability.

499. If the sun set on the 12th day while he was in Mina or had not left its limits, even if he was getting ready to leave, or even if he was travelling in a car but still within the limits of Mina, it is obligatory for him to observe the *mabeet* on the eve of the 13th, as well as performing the *Ram'y* – stoning – of the Jamaraat on the 13th day, and may not leave Mina before midday.

500. It is a priority for the [pilgrim] who is performing his First Hajj to observe the *mabeet* on the eve of the 13th too. This is also applicable to anyone who has breached some of the prohibited acts of the *ihraam*, or committed a major sin. In fact it is preferred for every pilgrim.

501. The necessary amount of *mabeet* is one half of the night, whether the first or the second half. Night is defined as from the Adhaan of Maghrib to Adhaan of Fajr. Therefore it is permitted for one to leave Mina after midnight if he had observed *mabeet* during the first half of night, although it is preferred to observe the *mabeet* throughout the night until Fajr.

502. It is obligatory to state the *niyyah* for the *mabeet* in Mina for the eves of 11th, 12th and 13th in the same way as in other duties and rites. *niyyah* should be stated after the time of 'Esha if he had not done so at the time of Maghrib. He should state, "I observe the *mabeet* this night in Mina seeking nearness to Allah Almighty". Abandoning [the declaration of] the *niyyah* constitutes a sin, but he is not liable to *kaffaarah*, although, as a precaution, it is *mostahab* to give one.

---

[36] and vice versa.

503. If one left Makkah but did not reach Mina or fell asleep on the way [to Mina], or he who had forgotten, or were ignorant of the ruling, or due to an oversight, or was overcome by illness or sleep, and therefore did not manage to observe the *mabeet* in Mina, he is not liable to anything. The same is applicable if there was no space in Mina to stay for *mabeet*, or if there was an excuse preventing him from observing the *mabeet* in Mina, such as fear of an enemy, or disease and such like.

504. It is permissible to engage in acts of worship in Masgid al-Haraam or the Mas'a [the route between Safa and Marwah], as a substitute for observing the *mabeet* in Mina. He could go to these two sites, and engage in acts of worship such as prayers, recitation of the Qur'an, reading various *Du'a* and supplications, seeking forgiveness – *istighfaar* – performing *tawaaf* and *sa'y*. Doing so for one half of the night seems to satisfy the requirement [of *mabeet*], having the choice between the first half of the night, which is from the Maghrib Adhaan until midnight, and the latter half, which is from midnight to the Fajr Adhaan. In that case, [the requirement] of observing *mabeet* in Mina is waved.

13. *Ram'y* of the Jamaraat

505. The thirteenth rite of the Hajj is the *Ram'y* of the Jamaraat in the Days of Tashreeq. It is obligatory to perform the *Ram'y* – stoning – of the three Jamaraat – Obelisks – on the days of 11th and 12th, and also on the day of the 13th if he observed the *mabeet* in Mina that evening. The three Jamaraat are the Sughra [Lesser], the Wusta [Middle], and the Kubra [Greater] ones.

506. It is obligatory to *Ram'y* (stone) each of the three Jamaraat with seven stones, as mentioned earlier in the section of the *Ram'y* on the Day of Eid.

507. It is obligatory to comply with the order of *Ram'y* or stoning the Jamaraat;

- First to stone Lesser Jamara, which is the closest Jamara to Mina,
- Then the Middle Jamara, which is the one after,

112

- Then Jamarat-ul-Aqabah also known as Kubra or the Greater, which is the one stoned on the day of Eid, last of the Jamaraat to be stoned.

508. If one stoned the Jamaraat without adhering to the order mentioned, say if he started with Jamarat-ul-Aqabah or the Wusta, he should repeat the *Ram'y* adhering to the order mentioned.

509. The time for performing the *Ram'y* – stoning – of the Jamaraat is from sunrise to sunset, which is the Designated time. It is permissible for the excused to perform the *Ram'y* during the nighttime under emergency circumstances, like women, the sick, the shepherd, the log collector, and the fearing (who can perform the *Ram'y* during the night instead of day). If the excused cannot perform the *Ram'y* on every night, then he can do so by performing the rites of the three nights in one night.

510. If one performed the *Ram'y* – stoning – of the Sughra Jamara for four times or more and then, due to oversight, proceeded to the next Jamara to perform the stoning seven times, it is satisfactory to amend for the missing throws. However, if he stoned [the Sughra Jamara] three times or less, he must repeat the stoning of the Sughra Jamara and then repeat the stoning of the one after it. If the deficiency concerned the third Jamara (al-Aqabah) he should throw to make up for the shortfall only.

511. If one stoned the Sughra Jamara, which is stoned first, four times or more, and stoned the second and the third Jamara seven times [each], it is sufficient for him to make up for the missing throws of the first Jamara, without the need to return to the second and the third [Jamara]. However, if he had stoned [the first] less than four times, it is obligatory for him to repeat [the *Ram'y*] of the three Jamaraat in [correct] order.

512. If he stoned the Sughra Jamara seven times, then [stoned] the second [Jamara] three times, and then [stoned] the third [Jamara] seven times, he must repeat the stoning of the second and the third Jamara seven times each, and he does not need to repeat [the stoning of] the first. If he stoned the second four times, but the first and third seven times each, it is

sufficient for him to make up for the missing throws of the second Jamara only.

However, as a *mostahab* precaution, in all cases one should repeat [the stoning of] all three Jamaraat if the order and continuity was breached.

513. If the Haajj forgot to perform the *Ram'y* on one of the days of Mina, or deliberately failed to do so, he is obliged to perform it – as *qadha'* – on the following day. He should start to perform the *Ram'y* for the day he has missed, and then [upon completion] perform the *Ram'y* for the current day. It is *mostahab* – desirable – to perform the missed *Ram'y* of the previous day [soon] after sunrise, and that for the current day by midday.

514. If he missed [the stoning] one of the Jamaraat, and he does not know whether it was the first (Sughra), or the second, or the Aqabah, he is obliged to repeat the stoning of the three Jamaraat in order, starting from the first, (the Sughra), then the second, and then the Aqabah. The same applies if he missed hitting a Jamara four times and he does not know which Jamara it is. If he missed less than four [times] for a Jamara, and he is not sure which one it is, he should repeat the *Ram'y* for the three Jamaraat, but order of the Jamaraat is not obligatory.

515. If he scored four and missed three, but he was not sure whether these [missed ones] were for one [Jamara] or more, he is obliged to stone each one of them [the Jamaraat] with three stones in order, starting with the first (the Sughra), then the Wusta, followed by the Aqabah. If he hit the target three times and missed four, he should repeat the *Ram'y* anew.

516. If one forgot to perform the *Ram'y* of the three Jamaraat, and entered Makkah but then remembered his oversight, it is obligatory for him to return to Mina to do so. If one did not remember his oversight until he left Makkah, he must perform it as *qadha'* the following year, or appoint an agent to do so on his behalf. If one deliberately failed to perform it, his Hajj is not corrupted and as a *mostahab* precaution he must perform it as *qadha'* the following year.

114

517. If a woman threw three stones, but then could not continue to complete [the Ram'y], if delaying for later on the day, and resuming the Ram'y was possible for her without difficulty, then she may not appoint an agent to do the Ram'y on her behalf. Otherwise Ram'y by proxy is permissible for her, provided the order and continuity [of the Ram'y] is maintained, as a precaution. If the woman delayed the Ram'y, and performed it as qadha' in the following day, it is considered qualified.

518. It is permissible for a woman to perform the Ram'y by proxy if she is apprehensive about the overcrowding.

519. If a sick person does not consider himself able to perform the Ram'y when it is due, if he picks the stones in his hand and someone else helps him to throw them he should do so. Otherwise he could do so by proxy. If the person concerned recovered during the period of Ram'y, as a mostahab precaution he should also perform the Ram'y himself.

520. If one completed the rites of Mina in the three days mentioned and performed the Ram'y in each of those days, he has concluded the rites of his Hajj, if he had also finished the rites of Makkah. He is therefore able to return back to his hometown. However, it is preferred that he returns to Makkah to perform Tawaaf al-Widaa' – the Farewell tawaaf – for it is mostahab.

The Mufradah Umrah

521. The Mufradah Umrah falls into two categories: obligatory, and *mostahab*. The obligatory one is of two classifications: fundamental obligation, and secondary obligation.

522. The fundamental obligation of the Mufradah Umrah: is to be preformed [at least] once, along with the particular criteria of the Hajj, as specified by the *Shar'*. The obligation of the [Mufradah] Umrah upon the people of Makkah, or those to whom the ruling of people of Makkah apply, is not conditional upon their ability to perform the Hajj as well, for they may be *mostatee'* – able – to perform the Umrah but not the Hajj, or the Hajj but not the Umrah, since the Hajj and the Mufradah Umrah are two different rites, independent of one other.

523. One who is remote from Makkah is not obliged to perform the Mufradah Umrah, but he is obliged to perform the Tamattu' Umrah and the Tamattu' Hajj. However, if he was able to perform the [Mufradah] Umrah but not the Hajj, then it is obligatory for him to perform the Mufradah Umrah, as a precaution. If he failed to perform it [The Mufradah Umrah] and died, as a precaution it should be perform as *qadha'* by proxy.

524. The agent who himself is not *mostatee'* to perform the Hajj, after finishing his proxy Hajj job, as an obligatory precaution should perform the Mufradah Umrah for himself, if he became *mostatee'* only to do the Umrah.

525. The secondary obligation of the Mufradah Umrah arises through *nadhr* [vow], promise, oath, hire, as a condition of a contract, or through corruption of the Hajj, or through missing the Hajj, where, in the latter case, he would only be released from the *ihraam* [of the Hajj] by [performing] the Mufradah Umrah.

526. The Mufradah Umrah is obligatory for one who wishes to enter the holy city of Makkah, since it is not permitted for one who wishes to enter Makkah to cross any of the *miqaat's* except by declaring and assuming *ihraam*.[37] As for the individual who wish to enter the Haram but not the

---

[37] and he can only be released from the state of *ihraam* by performing the Umrah.

holy city of Makkah, the likelihood is that he is not obliged to the Mufradah Umrah [i.e. he is not obliged to assume *ihraam*].

527. Apart from the obligatory grounds, it is *mostahab* – desirable – to perform the Mufradah Umrah once a month, and its desirability is emphasised during the month of Rajab.

528. If one performs two consecutive [Mufradah] Umrah – either in person or by proxy – the reward is greater if there is a time gap of ten days, than if there were less. In any case, the reward for them is great. If [one was performing] the two Umrah's for two different persons, then the issue of time gap [between the two Umrah's] would not be applicable.

The Rites of the Mufradah Umrah

529. The rites of the Mufradah Umrah are eight:

    I.   The *niyyah*.

    II. To declare and assume *ihraam* from one of the *miqaat*'s – designated locations – previously mentioned, if the adult passed by one of them. If one did not pass by one of them, he should declare and assume *ihraam* from his hometown, if it was outside the [borders of] Haram, but closer to the Haram than the *miqaat*. If the adult was within the limits of the Haram, he should then declare the *ihraam* from the borders of the Haram. As for the one who was inside the holy city of Makkah, he should leave Makkah for Masgid al-Tan'eem – al-Tan'eem mosque – to declare and assume the *ihraam* from.

    III. *tawaaf* of seven rounds around the sacred Ka'bah, as mentioned previously.

    IV. Two-*rak'ah* prayer of *tawaaf* by Maqaam Ibrahim or behind it.

    V. *sa'y* between Safa and Marwah.

    VI. *halq* or *taqseer*.

    VII. *Tawaaf al-Nisa'*, as previously mentioned in the rites of the Tamattu' Hajj.

    VIII. Two-*rak'ah* prayer of *Tawaaf al-Nisa'*.

The Rulings of the Masdood (The Barred)

530. The *Masdood* is he who is barred [from performing the Hajj or Umrah], after declaring and assuming the *ihraam*, regardless of whether this barring was at the two *woquf's* (Arafaat and the Mash'ar), if his *ihraam* was only for the Hajj, or he was barred from entering Makkah to perform the *tawaaf* and *sa'y* when he was in state of *ihraam* for Umrah, and thus not being able to perform the *tawaaf* and *sa'y* until their time had run out. In that case he should release himself from the *ihraam* by *Had'y*, i.e. by slaughtering the animal, at the place he was barred [from proceeding further on].

531. It is permissible for the *Masdood* to slaughter the animal before the day of Eid, and as a precaution, one should also perform the *halq* – shaving – on the same day too.

532. It is permitted for the *Masdood* to remain in his *ihraam*, and release himself from it by performing the Mufradah Umrah, which is by performing the *tawaaf* around the Ka'bah, then the prayer of the *tawaaf* by the Maqaam or behind it, then the *sa'y* between Safa and Marwah, then the *taqseer*, then *Tawaaf al-Nisa'*, and then its prayer by the Maqaam or behind it.

533. The *Masdood* has discharged his duty to the Hajj if he acted accordingly, as mentioned above, unless he had become *mostatee'* – liable to performing the Hajj in the previous year or before it [by meeting all the criteria required for the Hajj], or if he continued to meet those criteria in the next year(s).

534. If he managed to observe the two *woquf's* (Arafaat and Mash'ar) but from there he was barred from performing the rites of Mina – the *Ram'y* [stoning], the *Had'y* (slaughtering), and the Shaving/Trimming – if he was barred from entering Makkah and performing its rites too throughout the month of Dhil-Hejjah, the previous ruling applies to him.

535. If the barring covered the rites of Mina only, and it was possible for him to perform them by proxy, it is obligatory for him to do so, i.e. to

arrange for someone to perform those rites – stoning, slaughtering, shaving – on his behalf. On the completion of those acts, he is released from his *ihraam*, and he then should perform the rest of the rites. If he could not do them by proxy, and he was not able to find an agent to do them for him on his behalf, as a precaution he should slaughter his animal, and remain in his *ihraam* until he can be released [from it] by the Mufradah Umrah.

536. If he completed the rites of Makkah, which are the *tawaaf* and its prayer, the *sa'y, Tawaaf al-Nisa'* and its prayer, but was then barred from returning to Mina for the *mabeet* there for the Nights of Tashreeq, and for the *Ram'y* of the Jamaraat during their days, he is obliged to perform the *Ram'y* by proxy, and he could engage in acts of worship in Makkah during the nights of the *mabeet* in Mina, if possible. Otherwise, as a precaution, he should give a *kaffaarah* for not observing the *mabeet* in Mina. If it was not possible to perform the *Ram'y* by proxy in that year, he should do so in the following year, and his Hajj is correct.

The Rulings of the Mahsoor (The Sick)

537. The *Mahsoor* is the pilgrim who declares and assumes the *ihraam* for either Hajj or Umrah, and then falls ill such that he is not able to perform the rites, in a similar way to the case of the *Masdood*. If during the declaration of the *ihraam* he had made it conditional that Allah Almighty releases him [from his *ihraam*] if he were to be confined, he would then be released from his *ihraam* without the need to send his *Had'y* to the site [for slaughtering].

538. The pilgrim who had declared and assumed *ihraam* for the Tamattu' or Ifraad Hajj, the ruling above applies to him. However, if the pilgrim declared and assumed *ihraam* for the Qiraan Hajj, and had his *Had'y* accompanying him, he is released from his *ihraam* as soon as he sends his *Had'y* away [for slaughter] and he does not need to wait for the *Had'y* to reach the [slaughtering] site.

539. If during the declaration of the *ihraam* he had not made it conditional that Allah Almighty releases him [from his *ihraam*] if he were to be confined, he would remain in his [state of] *ihraam*, and as a precaution, he should send his *Had'y* for slaughtering, and when it reaches the [slaughtering] site, and the time of its slaughter had passed he could trim and release himself from *ihraam*. It is permissible to slaughter the animal in the locality [of the ill pilgrim].

540. It is obligatory for the *Mahsoor* to perform the Hajj again if he had previously met all the criteria for the Hajj requirements – become *mostatee'* – but did not perform the Hajj on that year. If, however, in the future years he did not manage to perform the Hajj himself, [he remains liable to the Hajj] and must do so by proxy.

541. If the pilgrim became *Mahsoor* in the *ihraam* of the Hajj, regardless of whether the Hajj was Tamattu', Ifraad, or Qiraan, the [slaughtering] site of the *Had'y* is in Mina. If the pilgrim became Mahsoor in the *ihraam* of the Umrah, regardless of whether the Umrah is Tamattu' or Mufradah, the spot of the *Had'y* is in the holy city of Makkah.

542. If the cause [i.e. illness] disappeared, the pilgrim should join his group to perform the rites. If he managed to observe the two sites of *woquf* (Arafaat and Mash'ar), or one of them, as mentioned previously –

about the obligation of performing [the rites of] these two sites[38] – he has complied with the Hajj, and he has not missed anything. If he does not manage to reach two or one of those sites, he has missed the Hajj, and thus he should perform the Mufradah Umrah and release himself from his *ihraam*.

543. If, due to his illness, he could not perform the rites of the day of Eid, and those after, he must perform the *Ram'y* and slaughter by proxy, and then perform the shaving himself, [i.e. not by proxy]. If he could, he should perform the *tawaaf* and the *sa'y* himself or with the help of others, otherwise he should do them by proxy too. He should say the prayer of the *tawaaf* if he was present in the [Grand] Mosque, otherwise, as a precaution, he should perform the prayer himself and also do so by proxy in its place [by Maqaam Ibrahim or behind it]. He should observe the *mabeet* in the Mina if he could, or engage in acts of worship in Makkah instead, and his Hajj is correct, otherwise he should give a *kaffaarah* for not observing the *mabeet*, as a precaution.

544. If due to sickness he was prevented from performing all the rites of Mina and Makkah, it is obligatory for him to send his *Had'y* [for slaughter], and release himself from his *ihraam*, and repeat his Hajj again if he still was *mostatee'* next year, unless he was liable to Hajj previously [and had not performed it, in which case, he must perform the Hajj next year regardless of him being *mostatee'* or not].

Prayers in Makkah and Medina

545. It is permissible for the traveller to the holy cities of Makkah and medina to perform his prayers 'complete'[39] in those cities, whether inside the Mosque or outside it, in the old city or in the new.

This is the last of what we wished to state concerning the rites of the Hajj and Umrah, for Allah is All-Knowing.

The Holy City of Qum

Sadiq al-Shirazi

---

[38] See case # 425.

[39] i.e. four *rak'ah* instead if two, where applicable.

PART 3 – Glossary

Bismillah al-Rahmaan al-Raheem

Aba	The usually black cloak worn by women in Arab countries as the means of *hijaab* or part of.
Arafaat	An area outside the holy city of Makkah and beyond Mina and Mash'ar al-Haraam.
Arafah	Day of *Arafah* is the ninth day of Dhil-Hejjah, when *woquf* is observed in Arafaat from midday until sunset in solitude supplication and intimate discourse with the Almighty. This day is considered to be of supreme significance to the extent that the hadith states, "the Hajj is Arafah".
Adhaan	The call to the daily obligatory prayers.
Adnal-hill	The nearest point to the Haram where one can be without *ihraam*, or the nearest point to the Haram where one can declare and assume *ihraam*.
al-Tan'eem	Reference to Masgid al-Tan'eem, or the al-Tan'eem mosque, which also serves as a *miqaat* for Umrah al-Mufradah.
al-Tashreeq	Reference to al-Tashreeq days / nights, which are the 10th, 11th, 12th of Dhil-Hejjah.
Anbar	A substance that releases scent when burnt.
Arafaat	A district outside the holy city of Makkah, where the pilgrim must observe *woquf* there between noontime and sunset.

awrah	Areas of the body that are obligatory to be covered. In the case of a male, it is area from the abdomen, around the navel level, to the knees. In the case of a female, it is the entire body.
Dhil-Hejjah	The twelfth month of the Islamic lunar calendar. Also written as Dhul-Hejjah.
Dhil-Qa'dah	The eleventh month of the Islamic lunar calendar. Also written as Dhul-Qa'dah.
Dirham	A unit of currency used during the Islamic era, which is still used as a currency unit in *Fiqh* discussions. Ten Dirhams is equivalent to one Dinaar, which is equal to one *mithqaal*, which is equal to 3.153 grams of gold. Thus one Dirham is equal to 0.3153 grams of gold, or one-hundredth of an ounce of gold.
Du'a	Supplication.
Eid	Festival / Celebration.
Fajr	The start time when the sky begins to lighten up. It is normally one-and-a-half to two hours before sunrise, depending on the geographical coordinates of the locality.
Farsakh	Unit of length measurement, which is about 5.5 km, or 3.4 miles.
Ghusl	The complete head-to-toe wash. Some *ghusl* are obligatory and some are optional. A *ghusl* becomes mandatory for both husband and wife every time they engage in penetrative sexual intercourse. It is also obligatory for a man if semen discharge occurs outside sexual intercourse. A *ghusl* is also obligatory for a woman after the end the menses period, before she can resume her various acts of worship.

Ha'edh	A woman who is experiencing the monthly menstruation.
Had'y	The Sacrifice that is offered on the day of Eid in Mina.
Hadath	Any discharge of urine, faeces, semen, or wind is referred to as *hadath*.
Hadith	Narration of the saying of the prophet or the imams *alayhum-as-slaam*.
Hajj	Pilgrimage.
Hajjar al-Aswad	The Black Stone, placed in a corner of the sacred Ka'bah.
Hajjat-al-Islam	The Pilgrimage of Islam.
Halaal	Permitted.
Halq	Shaving.
Haraam	Illegal, prohibited, forbidden.
Haram	The Sacred, or the Sanctuary. This is in reference to the area that encompasses the holy city of Makkah.
Haydh	The monthly menstruation period.
Hemyaan	A belt that is permitted for men to wear during *ihraam*.
Hijamah	Bloodletting or cupping that is performed in order to extract 'bad' blood from the body.
Hijr Isma'el	The stonewall of Isma'el, a few meters from the Ka'bah.
Ihraam	The state of consecration that the pilgrim assumes in which s/he refrains from a number of particular acts seeking forbearance, pleasure and adornment in humility before Allah Almighty.

InSha'Allah	By the will of Allah.
Istighfaar	Seeking forgiveness from Allah Almighty.
Jabirah	Wound dressing.
Jamaa'ah	Congregation.
Jamaraat	Plural for *Jamara*, the three obelisks representing the three appearances Satan made to Prophet Ibrahim *alayhis-salaam,* in an attempt to discourage him from executing the orders of Allah Almighty.
Jamarat-al-'Aqabah	Also known as the ***Jamarat-al-Kubra,*** it is the third obelisk – representing the temptation of Satan – that is stoned on the days of Eid and the following two days.
Janaabah	One is in the state of *Janaabah* whenever engages in sexual intercourse with one's spouse. A man is in a state of *Janaabah* whenever seminal discharge occurs.
Ka'bah	The cubic building that is the symbolic House of Allah Almighty. Also referred to as Bayt-al-Haraam.
kaffaarah	Compensation, atonement for breaching prohibited acts, or failure to do something obligatory. Plural *kaffaaraat*.
Khatam	Traditional ring.
Khums	Meaning one-fifth, Khums is the contribution of 20 % of the annual superfluous un-Khumsed income.
Ma'soomeen	Meaning the infallible or impeccable individuals, this is a reference to the Prophet Muhammad, his daughter Fatima, and the twelve imams, the first of whom is Imam Ali, and the twelfth, Imam Mahdi *alayhum-as-salaam*

Mabeet	Literally meaning to remain, this is one of the rites of the Hajj, which is required to observe in Mina.
Madhhab	Sect.
Maghrib	The time for *maghrib* prayer. *Maghrib* is the time when the redness of the central part of the sky, which is visible during the time of sunset, vanishes. *Maghrib* is some ten to twenty minutes after sunset, depending on the geographical location.
Mahram	Two people are said to be *mahram* if there is no *hijaab* restriction between them, like husband and wife, or mother and son, or father and daughter, brother and sister, etc.
Makruh	Discouraged, undesirable, etc.
Manaasik	Rites.
Masgid al-Haraam	The Grand Mosque, which houses the Ka'bah.
Masgid al-Shajarah	A mosque outside the holy city of Medina, which serves as the *miqaat* for the pilgrim heading to Makkah from the city of Medina.
Mash'ar al-Haraam	Also known as Muzdalafah, it is an area between Arafaat and the holy city of Makkah.
Meetah	Meat of an animal that has not been slaughtered in an Islamic way, or that has died or been killed in other ways.
Mina	An area in the vicinity of the holy city of Makkah where *mabeet* is observed.
Miqaat	A designated place that pilgrims must declare and assume *ihraam* from.
modd	A unit of weight equivalent to 750 grams approximately.

moqassir	*Moqassir* means one who does not know the ruling regarding certain aspect (of a religious duty) and he is aware of this ignorance or shortcoming and where to find the answer for, e.g. through certain books, references, or individuals with the appropriate expertise, but does not make the effort to seek the answer. In this way he has failed to discharge his duty. For comparison also see *Qaasir*.
mostatee'	Literally means able, and when used in reference to the Hajj program, one is considered as *mostatee'* if s/he is physically and financially able to perform the Hajj as well as meeting other prerequisites.
Mu'min	The faithful, the believer.
muhrim	An individual who is in the state of *ihraam*.
mostahab	Encouraged, desirable.
Muzdalafah	Another name for Mash'ar al-Haraam
nadhr	Vow.
nafilah	Literally meaning extra, or optional, it refers to acts of worship that are not mandatory for the individual to perform, but one is encouraged to do so, such as the *nafilah* associated with each of the daily obligatory prayers, or the Night *nafilah*, etc.
nagis	The definition of something being "filthy" or "impure" by coming into contact with a source of impurity, such as urine, faeces, semen, blood, wine, dog, pig, etc. Antonym of *taahir*.
niyyah	Literally meaning the intention, it refers to having or making the right intention for an act of worship and it is obligatory for any act of worship. Normally it is not necessary to

	verbally state the intention and it is sufficient that one make a mental note of act that one intends to do, unless otherwise stated.
qaasir	*Qaasir* means one who does not know the ruling of a certain aspect of a religious duty, but in fact he is not aware of this ignorance and naturally does not seek the answer to the case concerned since he believes that what he is doing is correct. Thus one should not assume that what he is doing is always correct, and ensure to check with reference books or expert individuals. As a matter of fact it is imperative and obligatory for the individual to learn and know all aspects that s/he may come across in the course of one's life concerning the relevant issues.
qadha'	If an obligatory act of worship was not performed when it was due, it must still be performed past its time as *qadha* or 'missed'.
rak'ah	A cycle or round of prayer in any of the daily prayers.
ram'y	Literally, it means to throw, and in the Hajj rites, this refers to stoning of the obelisks.
rukn	A principal element.
Sa'y	The Hajj rite relating to requirement of covering the distance between the mounts of Safa and Marwah, by walking or otherwise, seven times.
Safa	One of the two mounts – now almost vanished – in the vicinity of the Ka'bah.
sahar	The second part of the night, from midnight to *fajr*.
salaat	Arabic for prayers.

Salaat al-Tawaaf	*Tawaaf* prayer.
sawm	Fasting.
Shaam,	The area including Syria, Lebanon, and Jordan.
Shawwal	10th month of the Islamic lunar calendar.
Shi'a	Literally meaning *follower*, it is traditionally used to refer to the Muslims who follow Imam Ali *alayhis-salaam* as the leader of the Muslims after Rasulollah *salla-llahu-alayhi-wa-aalih*, in compliance with the order of the prophet. Rasulollah *salla-llahu-alayhi-wa-aalih* specifically appointed Imam Ali *alayhis-salaam* as his caliph and successor on specific instructions from Allah Almighty.
Sughra	The Lesser.
Sunnah	Tradition or teaching (of the prophet).
Tahaarah	The state of purity or being in a state of *wudhu*.
Taahir	'Pure' – as opposed to *nagis*.
Talbiyah	Means compliance, fulfilment, or carrying out the orders of Allah Almighty.
Taqseer	Trimming.
tawaaf	One of the Hajj rites, which is to walk around Ka'bah seven rounds.
Tawaaf al-Widaa'	The Farewell *Tawaaf*
Tawaaf al-Ziyaarah	Also known as the Hajj *Tawaaf*, which is the first rite of Makkah after Mina.
Tawaaf al-Nisa	The Women *Tawaaf*. It is obligatory to both male and female pilgrims, regardless of their age, status, etc. A husband would not be halaal to his wife unless he performs this *tawaaf*, and vice versa.

129

Tayammum	The means of attaining the state of *wudhu* by using earth or dust as opposed to water, where water is either not available or it is harmful to use.
wali	Guardian, heir
Warce	A kind of perfume
Wilaayah	authority and governorship
Wudhu	Ablution or the ritual washing required prerequisite for the performing of the obligatory daily prayers.
Woquf	The mandatory rite of 'being' in the two sites of Arafaat and Mash'ar al-Haraam as part of the Hajj program.
Wusta	Middle.
Zakat	Literally means purification, it is the religious duty of contribution of a rate of 1 – 2.5% due to nine items when over certain threshold. The nine items are Wheat, Barley, Dates, Raisins, Camel, Cow, Sheep, Gold, and Silver.

Made in United States
North Haven, CT
10 August 2022

22528700R00075